Some tips

FOR DIVORCED WOMEN ONLY

from ladies who've lived through it all.

- Allowing yourself the time to feel and cry, and the chance to meet, date and have sex with as many men as you want can help you meet the future more confidently and more capably.

- Don't discuss your sex life with your ex, your current lover or a likely candidate—and never, never make comparisons.

- Beware of strangers, blind dates—and husbands of friends.

- Be willing to change—try new places, new men and new positions.

- Begin your new life by giving yourself a beauty check-up, and by getting a medical check-up.

- Take the initiative by taking a vacation, following up on the men you missed out on when you were married. Start playing

THE RE-ENTRY GAME

The Re-entry Game

OR

"How's your sex life—
now that you're divorced?"

By Carole Sims

WARNER
PAPERBACK
LIBRARY

A Warner Communications Company

WARNER PAPERBACK LIBRARY EDITION
First Printing: December, 1974

Cover photograph by Cosmo

Warner Paperback Library is a division of Warner Books, Inc.,
75 Rockefeller Plaza, New York, N.Y. 10019.

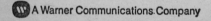 A Warner Communications Company

Printed in the United States of America

Contents

I.

What's the Story?

1. How's Your Sex Life?—Now That You're Divorced

The marriage lasted seven years. Then, after almost three thousand nights of sharing my bed with the same man, I was expected to sleep alone. Or was I?

Speculation and rumors had turned to fact. Word of our separation passed quickly among our friends and coworkers. Divorce is still News. And News gets reported, verified, discussed, and analyzed. Reactions were emotional; sides were chosen. I was pressed for details, offered support, and left with the words: "If there is anything I can do. . . ."

With more casual acquaintances, it was always the same. I brought it up (whether or not they had heard, it was up to me, some unspoken ritual). "You know, B and I are separated." No, I actually said *temporarily* separated; at that time I couldn't face the finality of our not living together. More reactions.

Then, as an announced divorced woman (really "separated" but few outsiders make the distinction, I found), I became public property. My sex life had entered the public domain.

Whether it was idle curiosity, sizing me up for a possible date, one-night stand, or lover; to proffer advice or admonish warnings, there was no holding 'em back. It was only a matter of time before I was hit with the big question on everyone's mind—primary, I confess, on mine, also—be it from friends, family, or total strangers.

Most were mindful of their manners and the question was posed in dozens of ways: How's your social life? Any men in your life? Who're you dating? What are you doing to keep busy? Got a boyfriend yet? Going to parties? Meeting men? You name it, I heard it. Over and over for about six months after the separation. It always came down to the same thing: Are you screwing? balling? fucking? Who are you fucking with? sleeping with? making out with? having sex with?

In other words, how's your sex life . . . now that you're divorced?*

From a married couple I had known for years: "Any particular man you're interested in?" Perhaps it was a kind of thoughtfulness on their part, but I regretted telling them whom I had gone out with the previous night, when they started to badmouth a mutual friend of ours—and told me the details of her sex life.

From a male friend who worked in the same office: "How's your social life?" When I said great, he looked disappointed. He never suggested anything but lunch but I'm convinced he didn't have the nerve to compete in an area where I seemed to have no complaints. Who knows what would have happened if I had said: "What social life?"

From a married couple I met at a party: "What's it like to be divorced and living in the city?" A notable ploy by an attractive, intelligent couple, and I responded

---

* I did have one friend who ignored my sex life for a real interest in my bankbook. "Are you getting alimony?" That was her problem!

openly about some of the difficulties. Pure naiveté on my part. Their "liberal intelligence" had been working overtime. I caught on when the next day I got a call from the husband, suggesting more than dinner. That whole conversation had been a setup: he, trying to find out if I was open to have a "little fun"; she, calculating her competition.

From a single female friend who had been at my wedding: "Have you met any interesting men?" *Interesting,* in her case, can be translated *fuckable.* Anxious to share my latest conquest with someone, I told all; and found her critical and unsupporting. Had my recovery been too fast? Was she jealous?

From a married friend with two kids and a husband who worked late: "It must be awful to sleep alone." Not having the guts to come right out with it, she made a statement. Whether she was really sympathetic, fishing for gossip, or projecting her future, I'll never know. Without acknowledging the question, I changed the subject.

From a first date: "How's your sex life?" My retort, "How's yours?" was out before I realized what I was saying. It led to graphic descriptions of three sexual adventuresses he claimed to be currently dating. Rather than turn me on, it turned me off. I wasn't up for that kind of competition—yet.

From a man I was sleeping with at the time: "Who else are you sleeping with?" I told him there were others. Such honesty wasn't exactly the way to keep him from getting uptight. It led to an argument and I never saw him again. I learned. Next time I was asked that question in bed, I said nothing. (I also made no false promises, either.)

From my soon-to-be ex-husband: "It must be difficult to meet the kind of man you've become used to, that you need." Hardly amazed that he should consider himself the authority on what I was used to (him), but frankly amused by his own estimate of how difficult it would be for me to find someone as good as he is—the bed included. But, simply stated, it was none of his goddamned business. Even under the best situations.

One woman I know who had been married for two years before she and her husband decided to divorce—and it was all very civilized—made the mistake of telling her husband about the man she met on her vacation. He never forgot, and when tempers finally rose at the final settlement meeting, sure enough, it was thrown back in her face. My answer to my soon-to-be ex, since I was feeling in a kindly mood, was evasive and ambiguous: "There's never a dull moment." Still, "none of your business" would have been more appropriate.

From a "sympathetic" friend of the family: "Well, when are you getting married again?" I saw through that one. Translated, this worldly provincial male was saying, "We know you have sexual needs so you'd better get married." My answer was standard: "I'll send you an invitation." But my feelings were aroused —resentment that marriage was supposedly the answer to "my problems," and pure anger that marriage was considered to be the solution to my sexual needs.

My family joined right in with the others. My parents were unpredictable. The night I called to tell them the News, my father went into his number: "Are you living with anyone?" Leave it to my father to go for broke, to start with his worst fears. Calculated to shock, I laughed. Even in those "most trying times" my father's blatant worries about his daughter's reputation were comical. If it had been a Shakespearean tragedy my father would have been used by the master to provide comic relief from the heavy proceedings prevailing. And since I was not living with anyone at the moment, having just given up a full-time roommate in the form of husband, I answered no. To which my father proceeded without preamble in his most inimitable way.

"Remember there are lots of men who take advantage of girls. And you have a big heart. So don't offer anything to them. And be careful of the man who takes you to lunch and listens to all your problems. You may think he is understanding and. . . ." Then, after the pause, he plunged: "You're a very generous girl, and

10

you like to give to other people." I couldn't help it; I started to giggle and I remember him concluding, rather lamely: "And men are only out for one thing. I know. I'm a man."

And after this long, complicated series of statements strung together in a highly dramatic way—a trial attorney can be very effective in his delivery without having much to go on—I realized that my father had just psychologically sewn up my vagina; I was once again a virgin, and to remain that way until I married again (God forbid if she doesn't, I'm sure he was thinking).

It reminds me of my good friend Amanda. Her father asked us about our social lives, didn't wait for an answer, and managed to blurt out his reservations about our planned trip to Curaçao for the weekend: "Are you sure it looks all right for two divorcees to be traveling together? Won't men get the wrong idea?"

Parents may be dear and wonderful people. But with their time-worn views, and still being hung up on "What will people think?" they still believe that nice girls don't fuck. And, after all, their daughter is a nice girl. That's the same reasoning that had a lot of us believing that men wouldn't marry us if we weren't virgins.

Don't underestimate the prejudices of our parents' generation. Recently a man told me I was all wrong, that if I were really the hip person that I affected to be, my parents wouldn't dare try to interfere with my life. "After all, you haven't lived at home for almost fifteen years and you were married for over seven." The women in the room laughed. Parents never stop trying to protect their little girls, and when they ask how your social life is, they really don't want to hear about your weekend with your newest lover. At least mine didn't!

And there are always the well-meaning relatives who have nothing better to do than take credit for predicting my "failure" (divorce). Being the only divorced female in the immediate family, everyone seemed to compare me to my divorced male cousin, who, I remember—even though he was years older than me—had a number of women pursuing him after his "freedom" (divorce). Now that he's married again, somehow he feels he understands my situation, so when I visited my family and ran into him at the local deli, I shouldn't have been surprised when he took me aside and said: "What do you do for sexual fulfillment?" Oh, I forgot to tell you—he's a doctor and everything he says sounds like it comes right out of a textbook. He may have been genuinely concerned or he may have just been plain curious, but I was not about to confide in him (I hadn't trusted him since he'd taken credit for fishing me out of the lake when I was six—and I was convinced he'd pushed me in in the first place). But then when I just smiled and evaded the question, I was hustled to the corner of the shopping center and given a lecture on the pros of masturbation. I'll never know what that was all about, nor what his point was, but I certainly wouldn't have gotten that unscheduled lesson if I hadn't just been divorced.

My aunt tried another ploy. She announced that her sister (my mother) was always the square one in the family and was uptight about life (that is, sex), and then proceeded to ask me: "Who are the men in your life?" Not content for me to have the last word by changing the subject, she realized that she wasn't getting any information from me, and finally conceded: "At least they should be from a good family." Mrs. Portnoy herself couldn't have done better.

There's one uncle whom I've always been fond of. He's a self-made man who really does have a sense of humor beneath his crude exterior. At least he had the guts to come right out and ask me: "Listen, getting laid?" For a long time I refused to give him a straight answer but because I liked him I kidded him along. It was really none of his business and he knew it, but it didn't stop him from asking. Then one day he asked in front of a group of people. That was too much. Isn't anything sacred? So I decided to call his bluff. "Yes, lots. Are you?" That was it. He howled with laughter but he never asked me again in public.

12

But Roberta's grandmother—an eighty-eight-year-old woman—surprised us most of all. Unexpected support comes from the strangest places. When she found out about Roberta's divorce, she called her long distance and came right out and said: "Are you sleeping alone?" Roberta was flabbergasted into silence, so her grandmother continued: "Sleeping alone when it's cold is no good for you. You find a man." So much for the so-called generation gap. There was one woman who knew what it was about.

Total strangers were not to be ignored either. And it seemed to me that for the next few months my sex life became *the* topic, and the conversation, now that I look back, always followed a pattern. Once I stated that I was separated, and then divorced—and it always came around to that eventually—the next question was, invariably: For how long? And when I answered two months, or three months (and once three weeks), the next question was predictable: Was I getting laid?

Eventually my sex life was my own business again (that's progress), when I had been divorced about a year. But before that I was an easy mark—and maybe I was a little too eager to be friendly.

It happened, yet again, stuck in an elevator on my way to see my lawyer. There were two of us—my company for the moment was a really very nice man on his way to a job interview. That my divorce became a topic was only natural. But I wasn't prepared for the response: "Tell me, what happens to respectable girls who were used to getting sex regularly?" I didn't know whether to laugh or cry. And he was really serious. He asked because he was curious, this was his big chance to ask the real question—it wasn't like I could walk away. It wasn't a line or a come-on, he really wanted to know.

I wish I could have told him that the concerned government had state-subsidized brothels that catered to divorced women, where I would find men who meet my every need. These virile lads would be subject to a legal draft, and no exemptions, either! All men must serve! For those who felt sex and marriage was a proper state of affairs, it would ensure the moral fiber of American life. Not to mention the woman's reputation. And everyone would live happily ever after.

But I didn't tell him my fantasy. Instead I burst into tears—getting stuck in the elevator was the last indignity I could bear. No, his question was. I blew my nose and looked at him. He was startled into a paralysis. And he was obviously embarrassed that he'd asked the question and that I'd reacted by crying. He apologized but I just started crying again. About ten minutes later the elevator started to move and I finally emerged shaken, bleary eyed, and very unhappy.

Another time it was at the airport. And I'll admit everyone was a little drowsy, as we all were seated on the floor of the American Airlines terminal waiting for a plane. Six hours late. It was the air-controllers' slowdown. The feeling of camaraderie was evident, and a young man on the way to visit his fiancée had attached himself to me and I was grateful for his company. "Tell me," he said—after we exchanged life stories— "what do you do for sex if you're divorced?" A little high on the night air, not to mention the drinks, I answered without thinking: "I fuck."

Then we both collapsed in giggles and he managed to acknowledge that he had never thought of it that way. We parted when his plane finally took off and I never saw him again. And it was probably the most honest answer I had ever given to that question.

Till now.

2. The Re-entry Game: For Divorced Women Only

The world didn't exactly stand still while I married and divorced. Then, as now, yesterday's truths are proved false today before we've even digested them. Attitudes, as well as scientific data, move with startling speed. And with television, radio, movies, books, periodicals, each new notion is communicated with unprecedented speed. We are then expected to accept,

14

change, and before you know it that which was once true is now revised, overturned, or discarded. That we try to keep up with these changes is the nature of the times.

But unlike the past, where a generation was considered time enough to assimilate new ideas and get used to them (like an old blue denim shirt), we have little time to make room for the new—testing, accepting, and rejecting. We have no time to adjust, feel comfortable, and then move on. That's a luxury we are no longer being offered.

Instead, we are trying to cope with people who represent generations of thought that cut across economic, social, and age groups. And we are paying a dear price for that acceleration: the confusion when opposing "generations of thought" clash. There is no longer a society with rigid rules and regulations to determine proper behavior. Areas of group sympathies blur; morals, lifestyles, and attitudes are developing at different paces.

Adults are being forced to be grownups. To make their own rules, and in doing so to take the full responsibility of their own lives—setting goals, making commitments, pursuing pleasures, feeling sorrows. That should be the ultimate freedom—making our own decisions for our own lives. But it isn't that easy. And nowhere is this clearer than when coming face to face with the status of a divorced woman—and her feelings toward herself.

Amanda and I became firm allies in 1969 when we both discovered we were in the midst of breaking up a marriage. We had known each other since high school, but our friendship really began at this time. We had both grown up in the fifties, married and separated in the early sixties, and found ourselves divorced in the seventies.

I was twenty-nine years old, married seven years, no children. She was thirty-three years old, married eight years, two children. And despite the differences—children being a major factor—our feelings about divorce were similar. We were both facing our re-entry

15

arated in the early sixties, and found ourselves divorced in the seventies.

into the world as something to be reckoned with, cried over, fought with, and, finally, understood. We always had something to talk about. We had to decide what kind of life each of us wanted, to make our own rules according to who each of us was and what our responsibilities, commitments, and priorities were. No longer required to live by those rules that others told us were absolutes, we had to find out for ourselves.

In the first place, with so many generations of thought (friends and family) struggling to be heard when it came to advising us and understanding us, we both agreed that we would never listen to anyone again— only to each other. (My father thought I should now return to my home town and marry the proverbial boy next door, having gotten New York "out of my system." Amanda's mother was appalled that she preferred to work as a part-time researcher and pay for a sitter than stay at home. One mutual friend thought she and I ought to buy a big house in the country and coexist with "others.")

In the second place, we knew that we were caught up in a constantly revised generation of thought toward women in general—questions about our social, economic, and sexual levels were already being raised. Where did we see ourselves in that picture? One needn't be a card-carrying feminist to have been influenced by the Women's Liberation Movement. With consciousness rising in general, we couldn't help realizing that the time for women to make decisions for themselves had been long overdue. At that time it was only the beginning. Since then Women's Lib has taken on a lot of connotations, but with careful thought I don't think anyone can disagree that it has freed many of us to at least decide what our life is going to be. And there were glimmerings of this even then.

In 1969 Amanda and I found that even we, married women who had prided themselves on being aware of the changing world, had a lot to learn.

We no longer had time to be philosophical. For

Amanda, economic equality was no longer an issue to be discussed with friends over coffee when child support from her ex-husband was barely covering expenses and she was frustratingly trying to find a job that would pay fair wages. Social equality had been a terrific idea when my husband had been my permanent escort, but it was appalling when I found myself expected to bring a date to a dinner party (or, for the more liberated hostesses, come alone). Sexual equality sounded good when we were both safely married but was a far more complicated issue than either of us thought, now that we had to go out and find sexual partners.

And if finally facing myself in order to decide what I wanted to do, what I thought I could do, and wondering if I could do it wasn't enough to confuse me, the world certainly wasn't helping me to accept my newfound freedom gradually. Every day I was faced with new books about sex—how-to, what-not, and why-not; alternate lifestyles were receiving prominent news coverage; sex clinics were not yet quite established but Masters and Johnson were certainly paving the way; all around me a sexual dialogue was beginning. And the dialogue implied a revolution. Was there a sexual revolution? Was it really that simple: could I get laid any time, anywhere, and suffer no consequences within myself or from others? Somehow it didn't seem that easy. How could I avoid the image of the sex-starved divorcee, loose and promiscuous, if I tried to satisfy those needs? I wanted my fair share of the action—that was clear—but could I get it?

And if it was difficult for me, Amanda's anxieties were magnified by her two children. What would they think about having a man, not Daddy, at the breakfast table? Christ, she was a nervous wreck before her first date, let alone facing having sex. If Amanda spent a weekend with a man while her kids were with her parents, how could she tell her parents—their credo having been "Men will only marry virgins"—let alone make sure she was a good mother to her kids?

And then there were times, late at night, on the phone, when we both wearingly agreed that remarriage

17

would be the answer to all our problems—and preferably that day. But we knew better. Remarriage at that time would have been based on fear of facing ourselves —not on the love of a man. Amanda and I looked around and saw how our friends, some recently divorced, were handling their right to determine their own lives. Some considered the possible alternatives as burdens—and promptly remarried. Others attempted to hang on to the old notions of what's proper at all costs (they were the women we usually dismissed by saying: all she needs is a good fuck). Others punished those who cared to think for themselves (Amanda and I), yet participated in the most clandestine, hypocritical affairs. Still others rushed in to embrace each new passing fancy as if that were the only, and final, answer. In their hurry to keep up, they failed to realize the strain of the push-and-pull quality of their lives. They pursued new lifestyles and images, reconciling nothing. Others seemed to be taking advantage of these times by experimenting, recognizing the evolutionary process of finding answers.

My re-entry was an evolution based on trial and error.

I was determined to find someone to bed with shortly after my husband and I stopped living together. Once that was accomplished, I seemed to go from one bed to another: what was I really doing? Making sure I was an attractive woman? Avoiding going home to an empty bed? Hoping that tonight would be the best yet? Trying to fall in love (and remarry)? Forgetting about all my other problems? Asserting the sexual me that had been lying dormant for so many months at the end of my marriage? Showing my husband that some men thought me a desirable woman? (But I went to great lengths to avoid him, his friends, and his coworkers so that he wouldn't know what I was doing. So much for the contradictions of my thinking at that time.) Was I trying to fill the empty void in my stomach? Get rid of my headaches when I thought about the future without my husband? Relieve the anger I had toward my husband for deceiving me with his long-term affair up till the time of the split? Show the world I wasn't finished yet—that I could still find men who liked me even though my marriage had broken up? Who knows? But my life had changed and I was an eager, if not hysterical, participant. Were the blurred nights of mediocre sex solace to the finality of breaking up a seven-year marriage? There were times when I felt it was hopeless; at other times I felt dirty or easy (and I was fair game, wasn't I?), and used, and finally angry. But then there were times when I felt beautiful (well, pretty!). Desired. Elated. Hopeful. Quiet. Sad. Glad. Enthusiastie. Exhilarated. Sexy. And eventually—it took about six months—I slowed down and looked at myself carefully. I knew that I was a woman. I had certainly been with enough men who had made me "feel," and in many cases it certainly hadn't been a one-way street.

When I look back and think that a number of times I almost gave in and gave up—and that meant agreeing to marriage—I weep with relief that I did not. I had no idea where I was, where I was going, what I was doing. That I played it out and found myself gave me time to mourn my marriage. That I did not settle while I was still changing freed me to find my place in the generations of thought. That I emerged a person who can determine with some sensitivity (and gut) who I am, what I want, what kind of man I like, what kind of man adds something to my life, what kind of relationship I want to work with and commit myself to, was possible only after having been through those months of ups and downs. Only then could I look at the future.

If you are recently divorced, you are walking right into the vortex of that whirlpool of contradictory information, ambivalent feelings, and moral bemusement. That you are feeling the very same turmoil inside of you as well is basic to the problem. And the way you handle it will determine your future.

When I made the step I felt like I was drowning. How about you?

The really astonishing revelation about that period of time immediately after the separation lies not in its uniqueness. I have talked to enough other women to know better now. These divorced and separated women* only confirmed to me that the special time period was strangely alike for most of us, no matter who we are, where we live, or how we choose to express it. In other words: the experiences and feelings about sex that I have heard about and felt myself have been peculiarly ordinary in their similarities. It is how we choose to deal with them that differs. And, like the other divorced women, I have felt:

- the eagerness to participate, particularly with the media convincing us of our unalienable right to sexual fulfillment
- the bewilderment when faced with rules of a new game
- the acknowledgment that some of the same old and dirty ideas still exist about divorced women—despite the media's insistence that sex is for everyone
- the panic when faced with the first time (Will I live up to the women I am now reading about?
- the self-hate the morning after
- the sheer physical pleasure of sex and the joy of turning him on
- the disappointment of feeling exploited (there are professional divorcee-daters)
- the temptation to remarry immediately
- the hope of being loved—if only for a night
- the anger when faced with yet another night alone
- the humiliation of not getting turned on (when you're already in bed)
- the shock of being pursued by the most unlikely characters
- the humor of the first time (long after it's over)
- the knowledge that your juices are running again
- the hopelessness of no available males within a fifty-mile radius
- the exasperation of trying to juggle the kids, your

* Many women have chosen "living together" rather than remarriage. That too can end. Since a legal document does not alter our emotions (proved over and over), much of this book reflects their feelings as well as the officially divorced or separated woman.

work, and a good night of lovemaking—or even a "good fuck"

- the exhilaration when he calls you a "great piece of ass"
- the reticence to fully accept and admit that you may have to have sex with a number of men before you can really respond

And the woman who has allowed herself the time to experience every possible emotion, to feel and cry real tears, who has taken every opportunity to meet, date, and have sex with as many different men as she wants, has emerged as a woman equipped with a firm belief in herself, capable of making her own decisions for her own future.

II.

The First Time

The first time isn't going to solve all your problems but it could be a very important event in your life.

And it is essential to have it over and done with as soon as possible.

Or, as expressed by one woman when I asked her about her first sexual experience after her divorce: "You better be straight about this topic. It can be the most important night in any divorced woman's life. It was mine. It's not the sex so much but how I treated what happened. It's how I dealt with the whole thing . . . what I thought about later . . . how I applied it to the next time."

And another woman stressed: "It's not what I thought it would be like. All I can say is from the very least learn from it, and from the very most, dig it."

By Now You Should Know What Sex Is

Remember when you lost your virginity? I do. I was terrified and curious, but finally I did it and every time afterward I enjoyed it more and more. Then I married. Later the divorce. Guess what? I seemed to have come full circle. I wanted to have sex with a man but I was terrified and curious. . . . But it really wasn't the same.

There is a big difference between the first time after a divorce and that moment years ago when you finally relented to "go all the way." Plenty has been written about the double standards of the fifties, with boys pushing girls to say yes, girls wanting to say yes, but everyone "knew" that nice girls didn't say yes. At that time sex was something the girls giggled about and the boys bragged about. And neither of them really knew what "it" was.

Well, now you know what "it" is: when it's good it's very very good and when it's bad it's horrid; and that's what you are afraid of now.

And It's Your Move

So, lady, the responsibility is on your shoulders. And that's probably a lot different from the first time years ago when your first sexual experience was limited to:

- your husband on your wedding night (there are more of you than some are willing to admit)
- your fiancé, who wouldn't dare *not* go through with the wedding after you made love, therefore your virtue was left intact
- your boyfriend, who swore his undying love before you'd let him near you without your pants on . . . somehow it helped to know he "loved" you
- or, finally, as a result of your determined efforts to find out what it was about (masturbating was wearing thin), and you were past twenty-one.

That was a surely sorry state of affairs. Puritanism and a false set of morals prevailed upon women to abstain until marriage; some gave in only to their boyfriends; others gave up and gave in . . . and got a bad reputation. For the most part, women did not have much choice.

It's different today. Women have the responsibility

for making their own decisions. And that couldn't be made clearer to a recently divorced woman. And for some that freedom of choice is a burden. There is no man to whom society points and says: "there he is—your first fuck." In fact the tables have been completely turned and, frankly, any man will do.

And therein lies the rub. Who should he be? Where? How?

Or, as Jackie put it: "If a man had come up to me out of nowhere as I was leaving the lawyer's office the day I signed the papers and said 'Let's fuck,' I'd have done it right then and there."

Rarely can it be that simple. But the difficulty is in making the decision to take the plunge, not the availability of willing men.

In answer to the question of who the first should be:

Sara: "Hell, just as long as he likes you."

Sandra: "I look at it this way: If he's someone who you will have dinner with and are willing to spend that time with him across the table, you may as well spend that much time with him in bed."

Pat: "My advice to the first time: someone you will never see again. This way you never have to think of what will he think of me while you're fucking. You can just enjoy or not enjoy but you can get it over with."

Thea: "I always look at the hands: if he has sexy hands, sleep with him."

Jane: If you like him, sleep with him: married, unmarried, rich, or poor, handsome or ugly. If you like him, can't hurt to sleep with him."

Lois: "Anyone who you meet through mutual friends, or at a party where you know most of the people. This way he can't be all bad because if he's a friend of a friend, and I assume you like your friends, why not?"

24

Wendy: "I don't know about you, but for me it's the chemistry, the spiritual chemistry that gets translated into the sexual. What I mean is, you can usually tell a good fuck when you see one. And if you see one, act."

And generally, it's the first man who asks . . . or says yes, if you ask.

Fran was lucky. It just happened.

"I went to the movies alone. And I don't even remember what the movie was. It was the night that my husband sent me a telegram saying that he'd signed the papers and they would be delivered to me the next day. When the lights came up I was feeling better but there were tears in my eyes. I'm blind as a bat anyway and by now, with the tears, it must have been a very sad, or a very happy, ending, and now I couldn't even see. And then a weird thing happened. There was a man who was up and out of his seat even before the end credits were over even though the lights were on in the theater. He had to crawl over my legs. You know there is never enough leg room in the movies. And I thought I recognized him. But who could tell, I could barely see. Anyway, he left the theater. And I followed shortly. And then just like in the movies it started to rain while I was in the theater. And I couldn't get to my car immediately because the downpour was unbelievable. And there he was. He couldn't get to his car either. And the words: 'It wasn't a bad movie, was it?' I'll never forget those words as long as I live. I looked up at the voice with the long hair wearing a levi shirt and pants that had crawled over my own levied legs a few minutes before. And then to be honest with you I stared at his crotch and then blushed and said: 'No. But my life is.' Then he looked as if he was going to cry. To make a short story even shorter, that night his wife was in Mexico getting a divorce. Neither of us could escape fate. So we went to bed. I wish I could say it was warm and tender. It wasn't. We were using each other and it was a fair deal. We took off our clothes and fucked. Let me put it this way: my memory of the night is not associated with warmth. It is one of HOT. We got through the night as two abandoned, lost souls, and we moaned and groaned, tearing at each other and rarely stopping until morning. . . . It was something. He fell asleep. Exhausted. I was wet, tired, and spent. I got up and went to the bathroom and cried and cried and cried. It was the best cry I ever had. I took a long hot shower, got into my car, and left his place. Something told me not to even write a note. There hadn't been ten words between us.

"That day I received one ounce of Joy. No card. I knew who it was from. And we never saw each other again. Oh, we've seen each other. And we've both nodded acknowledgment. And that's it. And I will always remember him. And I will always be grateful: I never had to worry or wonder about who would be the 'official first' in my new life. And that was the best cry I ever had."

Cynthia, who lived in a small town with a limited choice of "firsts," was climbing the walls. She was ready, willing, and able to get into bed with almost any willing male. But there just weren't any around who weren't the husbands of her friends. So she decided to take a trip and get it out of her system.

"I live in a small town. Granted it's not far from the city, but everyone there knew everything everyone else was doing. And I felt I was the month's topic of conversation. I just couldn't relax. I was involved in a project at the time and kept myself busy—so busy that I didn't even have time to think about sex let alone have it. But it would sneak up on me. Just before I went to bed, I would think about passion. And then I started dreaming of making tender romantic love. Every night it was with someone else. Finally I got the point. I had to get laid.

"I had a really good friend who had been divorced for about two years. I asked her if she wanted to go to Puerto Rico with me. I just had to get away. And

I guess in the back of my mind I thought I might meet some man, any man, and we could make romantic tender love.

"On the plane she brought the subject up. She told me to concentrate on finding a man. She had all the reasons why I should pick up someone. I would never see him again. He wouldn't know anything about me. No one would talk if I was worried about that. And if I was really bad, it wouldn't matter because I never had to see him again.

"I remembered this when one of the hotel guests sat down at our table when we were playing blackjack. I flirted outrageously. When I think about it I have to laugh. I must have been so obvious. It wasn't difficult at all. With my knees shaking and my heart pounding I went back to his room 'for a drink.' He wasn't such a good lover but I am forever grateful for the initiation to my new self. Thank you Puerto Rican lover, wherever you are."

And I have another tip. It's even better when you travel with a divorced friend, she knows the score and can help you. She's had the men she wants and is more likely to defer to your goal than a single girl friend will be. You could go alone but a little moral support is always a help. She's been there.

And yet another woman found her own solution by an excursion alone:

"I decided that my first fuck should be a man who didn't know my husband. Since I lived in a small town, that narrowed the field considerably. But I was determined to go to Chicago for the weekend. Once there, it wasn't hard to find someone to sleep with me.

"Sure I wanted to fuck. So when this guy I met at the bar in the hotel I was staying at suggested going back to his hotel, I said yes. I wanted to get the first time over and done with—that's one of the reasons I was in Chicago, wasn't it? And I didn't really care with who. We had dinner together and left to go to his room. Once there I was really in for it: after we fucked once—and now I realize there wasn't much foreplay but I was so excited about sleeping with him I didn't really have time to realize he was a lousy lover—he turned me over and said, "Okay, we're going to go at it again." Just like that. I mean, I am perfectly willing to fuck, make love, touch, play, over and over again—when it's good that's what usually happens. But this was different. It sounded as if he were making digits on his belt. I hesitated. I was ready to leave. And then he got tough. 'Oh, no,' he said. 'Where do you think you're going? Not so fast. I spent thirty dollars on you tonight and I'm going to get my money's worth.' I almost fainted on the spot. I knew I was with a loony. I just quietly got out of the bed and went to the bathroom, trying to pull myself together, sizing up the situation, and figuring on how to get out of there. I went and sat on the toilet, despite his cries from the other room: 'Come on, baby. I'm getting ready for you.' I remember every word he said, it was worse than a bad movie. I remember looking at the ceiling while I was sitting on the toilet and promising the crack if I got out of here without him touching me again I would clean my closets, stop screaming at the kids, be nice to my mother, and think good thoughts about the world—and that's pretty radical for me, especially at that time in my life. And it must have worked. I walked out of the bathroom, very deliberately, and got dressed as fast as I could without making it look like I was racing against time—which I was, how long would he allow me to get ready to leave before he tried to stop me? I saw the headlines in my head: 'Divorcee gets what's coming to her in motel room,' with a picture of me, bloody, dead, and mutilated.

"But all that was unnecessary. I walked out of the room, he mumbled something but didn't try to stop me. Fortunately we were on the main thoroughfare and there were other hotels around. One was very large so I walked over there and asked about getting a taxi. The man behind the desk gave me a funny look but he called. The taxi came and I finally made it back to the comfort and safety of my own hotel room. Shaken. I closed the door and started to cry. Really the first cry since the divorce. Finally I pulled myself together and started feeling pleased with myself. I *had* gotten laid."

I hardly recommend you go to a bar and pick someone up—but get it where you can, and if you do, be a little more discriminating (or stay at your hotel, where you'd be safer).

What's more, she did have a good cry. And crying is often the only thing you *can* do to relieve the pain or to mourn the marriage.

AND SOME OTHER HORROR STORIES

There are other horror stories when it comes to the first time. Some men will expect you to be an acrobatic whiz while you're still trying to figure out where to put your legs. Others are the run-of-the-mill bad lays . . . that you have not yet been able to size up and say no to.

I have one friend who met a common-variety creep exactly two weeks after her husband left her. Terrified but determined to get into the sack, she agreed to spend a weekend with him.

"He seemed like a nice enough guy. He was a lawyer with a big law firm in town and he asked me to spend the weekend with him and some of his friends. So I went. As we were driving to the country his conversation took on a dirty undertone. You know . . . little childish innuendoes. I couldn't believe my ears. It seemed that's the way he got his sex too: by innuendo. In the total dark; in total silence; and no acknowledgment that I was the same person who had discussed the world's problems with him. And we got into bed. He just took me by the shoulders, kissed me sort of on the lips, pushed me down onto the bed, and rammed himself into me. One two three. It was all over for him. He then turned over and went to sleep. I wept for the rest of the night. I didn't know if it was me or him. I know I felt just terrible. So much for Instant Sexual Liberation people. I just wanted to go home. Even my husband looked at me when we had sex.

"When I had been invited away for the weekend with this guy I was scared. But I went—I had to get it over with; the first time. Well, I did. And as I said, it was really bad—even degrading. But I felt freed. In the last eight months I have made it with more men. Some were really awful. Others were good, and some were great. Through it I realized one thing: lousy sex life. I had slept with two other men before getting married. Now that's not much in the way of experience or getting to know what men's bodies are all about. Now I really think I can say I know men's bodies. And from that I know my body better. Now when I meet a guy I can usually predict what kind of lover he will be; at least I can avoid the losers. What's more, now that I know my own body, it sort of gets transmitted to the guy. And then he wants to get to know it too. It's funny how that works."

Don't be surprised if your reflexes aren't fast enough to avoid certain men who are less than honest.

Linda had been separated about six weeks and was admittedly looking around for the proper candidate to pop into bed with. She agreed to attend a conference given by the librarians' association. And there she met a man. He was charming, entertaining, witty, and, to Linda, sexy. He listened to her talk about her divorce and he laughed at her stories of trying to make it alone. It was only natural that they spend the night together.

"I went to my room first. And then about ten minutes later he followed. There we were bed to bed. There was no way to avoid the obvious. I mean I knew I wanted to sleep with him. He was the first man who even offered since the divorce. But I did feel pretty strange in a hotel. He suggested we take a shower together and it turned out to be a terrific idea. It really relaxed me. I felt that I didn't have to plunge right in and fuck. The whole thing was perfectly wonderful. After the wham-bam-thank-you attitude of my ex, this man was giving, loving, and we touched and played with each other for a long time before he went into me. And then he didn't come right away. He let me come. And then still erect, he pulled out and we played some more. It went on for hours: he ate me; I sucked his cock. Finally I got on top and wham, we both had the most sensational orgasm. Dynamite. I was in love. He left my room just before dawn and I fell asleep peacefully for the first time in months.

"The next day was full of meetings and I didn't see him although we had made plans to see each other the night before. Then my whole world came crashing: one of the women who worked at the library in his home town got very chummy with me when we took our break for lunch. And then she dropped her bombshell. My true love was married with four kids. It's not that I wouldn't have slept with him if I had known he was married, but he never, not once, mentioned it. I felt cheap and used. Maybe if my husband hadn't always been sleeping around I wouldn't have reacted so violently. I had been the wife for so long that I didn't want to be the cheap whore who slept with married men like the women who had slept with my husband. I've modified that now but at the time I was sick. I really felt that he had gotten to me, saw me vulnerable, and struck home. He just didn't have to come on as Mr. Available and this is for keeps. I'm an adult. I would have accepted it as an affair.

"I excused myself from the afternoon early meeting and spent the hour or so crying in my room. Then I put on new makeup and went back to the meetings. When I saw him later I may have been melodramatic at the time but I was so damned angry. Angry at him for deceiving me. Angry at myself for having been fooled. And I refused to see any more of him. I just can't stand anyone who lies to get what he wants. And he didn't deny that that was exactly what he was doing."

The first time for Linda was great in the bed and terrible for her head. She probably would have been able to spot him as married, if she hadn't been out of practice so long. That he lied to her was his mistake: he didn't think that she would have slept with him if she had known about his family. That's where he was wrong. No matter. At least Linda got the first time over with.

SHOULD I TELL HIM?

Once you make the big decision that this is *it*, it's up to you to decide whether or not you want to tell the man it's the first time (yes, life is just one big decision after another). For some woman that's no problem. If the man has known you or you have a chance to talk about your lives, it may be obvious. Some men can even be incredibly perceptive when it comes to making it easier for you.

Jennifer is a case in point:

"The first time was with a guy I met at a PTA meeting. His son and my daughter were both in the same school. And he was without wife and I was without husband. And there we were organizing the parents for some dumb thing so their children wouldn't have to eat their lunch in fifteen minutes instead of forty-five. His wife was God knows where and my husband was living it up in Mexico with his newfound love. Well, one night the two of us were arguing over the way we were going to present our demands to the school. We were at my place. And fortunately my daughter was at my mother's for the night; so it must have been a Friday night. And as far as sex was concerned, I just figured I would spend the rest of my life masturbating. I had been divorced for four months and it was so much just to keep Kathy—that's my daughter—from mourning the disappearance of her father, I just couldn't even think about men.

"And there was Larry. Good old Larry. And there was me. Good old me. And he kissed me and I thought, Where's Kathy? Then I realized that she wasn't there. And you know, I don't know whether or not I was relieved. Maybe I had been using Kathy *not* to face the fact that I would have to have men friends, date, have lovers, whatever you wanted to call it. After all, I was only twenty-eight years old then. And I couldn't really believe that I would be without any male attention for the rest of my life. And yet I did nothing to pursue it. All for Kathy, I said. But maybe I was just too scared.

"So, enter Larry. Who had been divorced. The second thought in my mind after Where's Kathy? and I knew that this was it: should I tell him that I was scared to death or should I try to carry it off that this was just like any other night that I would be making love with a man. I mean, just because I tell him that he is the first since husband, it doesn't mean that he will have any additional comfort or security to offer. I wouldn't count on that with the jerks I have known before I was married and since my divorce. On the other hand, if I tell him that he is the first, he may even get really uptight about it. And yet I reasoned very fuzzily at the time: I realize that this sounds confusing but all these crazy thoughts went through my mind at one time. You know how they say your life goes before your eyes just before you die: well, my alternatives went before my own eyes at that moment that Larry kissed me—with passion. And I might add it wasn't a quick peck. More like the slow-motion long-term kiss. So I had lots of time to think. At least three minutes.

"And so: Where was I? If I didn't tell him and I was weird or something then what would he think? That I'm weird. Well, I didn't tell him and I didn't not tell him—he made it easy: he asked me if he was the first. And I nodded my head. That was it. And it was fantastic. Wonderful. I knew him pretty well outside the bed and it was just natural to get to know him under the covers. And the same for me. In fact, we saw a great deal of each other later but that's not what you want to know. So that was the first time: I found my first love after my divorce through the PTA."

However, there are no guarantees. Even if you tell him that this is the first time you have been with a man other than your husband for the last five years, consideration for you might not be part of his style, at any time. One woman told the man she had been seeing that it was her first time, expecting some special treatment or care for her feelings. They made a kind of love, she told me, but she really doesn't remember the details—but she did remember the outcome.

"After he had his orgasm—I had mine—he just rolled over to his side of the bed and said good night. I was all ready to be cuddled, hugged, anything. I needed the touch and I also could have used some reassurance that I wasn't just a lay. I really took all my guts and said: 'Will you at least hold me for a minute?' He said: 'I never can get to sleep if I'm holding a woman.' Then he went to sleep, figuring that had closed the issue and I stayed up half the night figuring out a slow death for him and then wondering if it was because I was a bad lay that he wouldn't hold me. And in the morning when he woke up and turned to me I let him have it: 'How could you sleep all night long with me in bed and not touch me once? Don't you like me?' He answered: 'Baby, I told you, I have to sleep by myself. I can't touch anyone and it has nothing to do with how much I care.' That bastard couldn't revise his pattern even once when I was terribly needy. So a lot of good it did to tell him I was frightened and nervous."

So much for his warmth and understanding. She did see him a few more times (and had sex) before she finally called a halt—but she had gotten laid.

Although I've only heard it happen once, there's a chance he might get turned off if he knows it's the first. Vicki told me she took the chance and lost before she knew what happened.

"I wasn't too choosy when it came to the first. I was, in a word, desperate. I had been married for six years, divorced for three months, when I finally decided it was time to move to L.A. I had been living in the country in northern California and I thought my life would be less isolated if I moved to Hollywood Hills, where I had a lot of friends. And it was, I won't deny that. A friend invited me to a party and I went. One man was very interested and we danced and talked and I told him about myself—divorce included. We were necking a little, holding hands, and

I really figured this was it. When he asked me if I would spend the night with him I said yes, and then added that he would be the first man since my husband. He sat up and looked stunned: his vibes changed: 'nothing doing' seemed to be the message. He was very nervous all of a sudden, then gave me a whole speech about how we shouldn't sleep together because it didn't mean anything to him and I would no doubt hang a lot of meaning on it and get hung up on him. I only wanted to get laid, and squelched the desire to tell him he was only a sex object to me. The more he talked the more he turned me off. I let him go on and on and then I got up to leave—alone—and said, 'Thanks for . . . whatever.' "

Vicki told me she had to wait a week and another party to finally have sex—and this time she didn't take any chances. She didn't tell him anything about herself, let along being a three-month divorced woman. And according to her, "All went well." Cryptic. But I got the message.

And some women don't feel they want to let anyone in on their feelings—their pit in the stomach. One woman I know brazened it out. In fact, she went out of her way to find someone who didn't know her and probably would never see her again. She met him at a party, he lived in England, and was in the U.S. for only a few weeks. Perfect for her. She told me she was glad she did it that way because that way she could be selfish and not worry about whether or not she was doing it right. I questioned her about this and she finally said:

"He was really a damned good lover and it turned out that I wanted to give to him. But I was so afraid and I didn't know what to do. He was very aggressive and took over. I really had chosen well. I meanwhile felt miserably clumsy, all the time I seemed to be responding to his touches. I would go from really digging it to wondering what the hell I was doing. The upshot: I must have been a miserably self-absorbed partner and I'm sure he thought I was crazy. I obviously had some-

35

thing on my mind and that of course led to not being really involved—what was on my mind was, what do I do next?—and that led to little real satisfaction."

She confessed to me that that was part of her style, though. To fend for herself; not ask for help and hope for the best. She said that she doesn't regret a thing, because the next time, she was able to stop thinking and start feeling.

NO EXCUSES!

Now that you have been given the go-ahead to sleep with any man you want, don't make excuses for remaining in the psychological nunnery.

One woman kept coming up with candidates and putting them off because she couldn't be sure of the outcome. She wanted guarantees that bells would ring and the bombs would burst. There can be no assurances. And if you look for them you're bound to be disappointed. She was when she finally made her choice. With three months of hesitation and build-up, she was miserable when she finally said yes. Whether she gave it a chance, she doesn't know. But it was three months before she said yes again. And a pattern was set. It wasn't until she went to a therapist that she was able to work things out.

Noel might still be saying no if opportunity hadn't reared its head. She was twenty-nine years old, an attractive redhead, bright, and mother of two kids. Every time she met a man she worried so much about whether she should or she shouldn't, she convinced herself that no man turned her on. When she did go out she was paralyzed by indecision by the end of the evening. Then her own sexual feelings took her by surprise.

"I made it with the plumber. I know it sounds awful, like a bad joke, but I did. He came to fix the water pipes that had been clogged by a tree in the backyard. The kids were both at school. I was horny. He was damned sexy. I hadn't slept with a man for months. I found I was reading more and more about sex so I

36

wouldn't forget what it was. I'd go out but the antici-pation of actually *screwing* put me so uptight. So this plumber solved all my problems. There simply wasn't any time to anticipate. We did it right there in the kitchen. I don't necessarily recommend it for the first time, but it did the trick for me. He certainly wasn't one of these men who digs giving the woman satisfac-tion. Just picked up my skirt—it was summer—pulled down my panties—over my ankles—unzipped his fly, and was in me. It wasn't that satisfactory an experience *sexually,* but I got exactly what I wanted. Somehow, for some reason, that made me less afraid of sex. I may have used him but I figure it was an even deal."

And certainly afterward, Noel was less uptight when she did date and didn't have sex, sex, sex on her mind all evening. So when it came time to make the decision of whether or not to sleep with him (or make plans for it at a future time, depending on her kids' schedule) she was more assured of her own feelings and was re-laxed enough to allow herself to get turned on.

Donna kept putting it off because she felt inexperi-enced. She had been a virgin when she got married.

"My first time was a mind-blowing experience. Imagine, I had only slept with one man. My husband. I had been married in 1961, right out of college, and although I seemed to have done everything else, we didn't fuck. We got divorced in 1970. Nine years with the same man. Even if I had entertained affairs, I never had the nerve. I had no confidence in myself whatsoever when it came to the bedroom. I started dating after the divorce and one guy really turned me on. I saw him a couple of times a week and I kept thinking: 'I want to sleep with him, but what if he thinks I'm not good enough? Thank God, he was a sensitive man who understood a little of what I was feeling. He hung in there and finally he got me to trust him. I guess it was his persistence. He finally made me feel that I could do no wrong and even if I did, it wouldn't matter. The scene was set. I agreed to go away with him for a weekend. I knew this was it.

So did he. And by going away we cemented the intention. I mean, in a motel room, there isn't anywhere to run.

"We checked into the motel—it was during the summer and the motel was right on the lake. Then we went to dinner, and I was so nervous. But when we went back to the room, I knew this was it. We watched television and we cuddled. We necked. And he very, very slowly and methodically warmed up every part of me. He was so good, really. Finally, when he had our clothes off, he still was gentle, but very firm, and didn't scare me. As I got more excited, he became more forceful. If he had moved right in on me, that would have been it. But he was too smart for that.

"I felt comfortable and relaxed. I really trusted him. And from there it was truly wonderful. When he finally went inside me after what must have been hours of foreplay—kissing, touching, talking—I really wanted him. Very much. And all of a sudden, before I knew it, I started getting tense. I was so turned on. I felt like I could come all over the place in a matter of minutes. And you know, I did come. It was unbelievable. I never came so easily when I was married. But I really was able to let loose. And I trusted him implicitly. We stayed in the motel room for most of the weekend and got better and better. He was a damned good teacher and I was very lucky."

After this experience, she knew there was a lot for her to learn, but she was better able to cope with it.

The fear of the unknown shouldn't prevent you from saying yes. Rochelle wasted a lot of time worrying about it.

"I really wanted to break out and find someone to fuck but every time I started to say yes, I would pull back. I knew I could excite my husband. How did I know if I could even get a rise out of the guy I was with now? I mean, I didn't know him. I guess I was frightened of the unknown—wouldn't take the risk. With my husband I knew exactly what to expect and I knew what was expected of me. I had read so many books about all the things that could be done, and frankly I hadn't done half. How would I know what to do?"

When she finally said yes, she knew exactly what to do.

When the door closed on her marriage, Irene remembers hearing from her husband: "You move like a water buffalo in the bed when it comes to sex." Whether he actually said that doesn't matter. What does is that she really felt she was a terrible lay. And she was terrified of having sex. What she didn't realize was that he may not have wanted to sleep with her but that didn't mean she wasn't a desirable woman and could be good in bed with another man. He had associated her with a bad marriage—and being naturally cruel he was verbally abusive. When I talked to her (about four weeks after her divorce) we discussed this whole fear she had. She agreed to try, and is now vacationing in the Virgin Islands with, in her words, "a truly great fuck."

Irene's experience is not uncommon although it takes different forms. Moreover, it's usually subtle, but the message is clear: you are bad in bed. That accounts for why he no longer can get it up in his mind; in fact, it's a reflection of something wrong in the marriage or relationship. In some cases, however, the woman buys the line and turns the tables. She blames her bad sex for the divorce. Janet felt that way when her seven years of marriage broke apart. She was terrified to say yes. In her head sex would ruin everything.

"We had a good sex life in the beginning. A tapering off and finally nothing. He told me in effect that I wasn't a woman to him. That he loved me but I just didn't turn him on anymore.

"How could I ruin a perfectly charming relationship with the man I was dating by going to bed with him? I lived in stark terror that I would get into bed and he would throw up. Or make excuses. Or worse, try his very best . . . not to hurt my feelings. So

I made every excuse in the book not to get anywhere near a bed, bedroom; I even refused to see X-rated movies. That lasted exactly two weeks and four dates and I finally took the step. I was scared to death. But I finally whipped into bed so fast he never had time to see me naked. We had been necking in the living room and he suggested we move to the bedroom. While he wasn't looking I whipped off my clothes and got under the covers so fast, it's a wonder he didn't think I was crazy and leave right then and there. But he followed. And proceeded to caress every part of my body. Even I could tell in my state that he *liked* what he was doing. And his cock was so big it was obvious that I was *not* a turn off. What a relief. Somebody really *wanted* me. And that really turned me on. I finally stopped thinking and just started feeling. What a night."

She left that bed feeling like a desirable woman for the first time in over a year.

Turning off works both ways. Just because sex with your husband had evolved into something to be dreaded is no excuse for avoiding sex now.

When Gayle and her husband were first married, they couldn't seem to get enough of each other sexually. As their marriage began to draft into a truce between them rather than love, she found that when he touched her she was repulsed. She turned off her sexuality altogether. Eventually the marriage broke up, and Gayle felt that she was turned off forever. She was afraid to have any sexual experiences—or even think about them—because she didn't want to face what she thought was a problem. She thought she was, in her words, frigid. That no man would ever turn her on again. Fortunately for her, a man was interested enough in her to pursue her until she said yes.

"And then when I said yes, finally, it was fantastic. This guy really dug my body and I was really into it. I was nervous and he knew it but somehow it heightened the excitement for both of us. And I knew that I was a woman to him and I found myself responding to him and by instinct touching him in ways I had never felt free to do with my husband. That freed me. I knew I was a woman. One thousand percent."

Nothing like chemistry to get the juices running again, is there?

Don't fool yourself that you're turned off to men forever. An old school chum, Brenda, went into a whole number about her soon-to-be ex-husband. That he was the only man who ever turned her on. In her mind, life with him was shitty but the sex had been super. When they agreed to split, she informed me, she had had it with men, forever. Her own sense of drama was helping her deal with her pain. But I had no idea she was taking herself seriously. About six weeks after she split, she decided to take a weekend holiday to the Caribbean. Her grief obviously was not that debilitating. I got a hysterical phone call from her about a month after she returned from Puerto Rico.

"I'm pregnant." That's some way to be greeted before I had had coffee in the morning. But rising to the occasion, I tried to make some sense out of her by asking the natural question:

"By whom?" I wasn't going to give in until I satisfied my own curiosity.

"All right. When I was in Puerto Rico I met this man and . . . well, he was a damn good fuck."

"That's no excuse. But you can't be pregnant. You've been on the pill."

I wasn't worried, yet and I was glad that she had found a man she could turn on to—not that I doubted it for a minute. But the silence was beginning to bother me.

"What are you not saying?" I asked in my best therapeutic voice.

"I stopped taking the pill two months ago. I really didn't see the need. Since I hated the thought of sex, it seemed silly to take the pill."

So much for her facing the facts of life. She went to the doctor, she was pregnant, and she arranged for an abortion. Living in New York City, where abortion

41

on demand* is available, did make things easier for her. But it was an experience she could have well lived without . . . and could have just as easily avoided. She faced a basic fact of life: you never know when you're going to get turned on.

Be prepared for the unexpected.

Liz was really an organized, competent woman. But even intelligent women can overlook the obvious and suffer the consequences.

"It just never occurred to me to take my diaphragm with me when I flew to Mexico for the divorce. Who knew that I would have to stay over because of some legal mix-up? Who knew that I would wind up in bed with a man—whose name I can't even remember today? Who knew that I would end the three-month celibacy between separation and divorce in a hotel room in Mexico? It did occur to me at the time that I might get pregnant. But one lousy fuck. The odds were against it and I was feeling no pain. Okay, you already know the punch line. I did get pregnant and once again I was on the plane to patch up my life: this time for Puerto Rico for an abortion."

Both Liz and Brenda were actually going through strong emotional changes around the time of their divorces. A psychotherapist would have to tell them why they threw caution to the proverbial winds. At least in both cases this one lapse was enough to pull them back to reality and both are surviving quite well as divorced women.

* The Supreme Court has ruled that a woman is allowed to have an abortion on demand, which means the degradation of finding an illegal abortionist should finally be over. That abortion is a viable option to having a baby is each woman's decision. That it is now possible to get an abortion without jeopardizing your life is civilized. All the women I spoke to who had gotten pregnant after separation chose to have an abortion, illegal or legal. And in all cases, the abortion took its toll in a psychological and emotional way. It is not an easy answer . . . but at least an alternative. It is the woman's choice.

WHAT YOU CAN EXPECT

The first time is not necessarily going to be the most gratifying experience of your life. But you have to face it nonetheless without thinking that there is something wrong with you. Here's Janice's tale:

"I was all primed to make the first time something beautiful. Such are the ways of naiveté. One man who was pursuing me the day the papers were signed was going to be it. I prepared for the evening carefully. Made sure everything was staged properly.

"I wore my sexy new underwear, and then I decided to wear something casual, in other words: easy to get off. I put in my contraceptive. No sense in getting pregnant and playing out another scenario. I put all my goodies in a purse just in case we went to his place after dinner: perfume and clorets. What else did I need? A little money—mad money like I take on all dates—clean hair, and a wicked heart. I was ready. It was just like I planned. Until we got to bed. Mr. Generous with his money was Mr. Stingy in the bed. He read all kinds of books and he put up a good talk about making sure a woman was satisfied. But he sure didn't know anything about putting that into practice. Once we got into the bed, he aimed for the clitoris, gave me about ten seconds to warm up, and the next thing I knew he came inside of me (I don't even remember him going in, I was so pissed at this point). Then, with a casual kiss, he rolled over and went to sleep. I could have died on the spot. So much for the liberated male. At that point there was nothing I could do but turn over and go to sleep. Furious."

But she tried again—another man—the next week and it was even better than she had dreamed.

Candice found out the first time is sometimes more a feeling than sexual fulfillment.

"My first experience was with this guy in my office whom I had known for years. We went to lunch a lot. And I listened to him for hours when he talked about his divorce. I knew all about him. I even knew about some of his sexual hangups. His wife just couldn't make it—I mean, she just couldn't come. He was really frustrated. We went to dinner a lot when my husband was 'working late.' I knew there was an attraction but he was dating a lot and I was so busy trying to keep my marriage together. Anyway, he was one of the first people I told about David and I getting a divorce. Naturally he wanted to hear all about it. Even though we were good friends I really didn't talk much about my marriage so when I announced that David had flown to Mexico it came as a surprise. We went to dinner that night: I had two vodka martinis, and I rarely drink. I talked and cried a little and then he took me to his place. We sat for a while just looking at each other. Then he began kissing my lips. I couldn't believe it. I responded. He left my lips and moved to my neck and from there to my breasts. I was breathless and scared and simply amazed that I was responding. His lips were moist and moving. THIS WAS ONLY THE BEGINNING. We gently caressed each other and I felt tingling all over. I just curled up up in his arms. I even told him I was scared. You know what happened? I fell asleep. I woke up a few hours later and found myself in bed and we were both holding each other. I felt so tender to this man. It couldn't have been better."

The amazement of finding yourself in bed with a man who is not your husband is sometimes so overwhelming that the shit-eating grin isn't because you have had an orgasm but because you know what to do in bed . . . having sex. Agnes amazed herself:

"I was home wondering whether to end my life or go back to my husband when a friend of mine called and literally told me to go to this party with her. I really didn't want to go but the line of least resistance was to get dressed and be ready when she picked me up. I was not there consciously looking for a man to go to bed with. I was there because my friend told me to be ready. But probably looking back I was there for that purpose. Christ, it had been six months since

I had had any sexual relations with any man. I had been separated two months and the last four months of marriage was ice-cold between my husband and I.

"So we arrived at this gorgeous loft fixed up by some people in the art business. Most of them were oohing and ahing about my new status in life: FREE. In the midst of one hysterical repartee—it was that kind of party—one man came up to me and asked me to dance. There was a good live rock band there. Anxious to get away from shouting about my alimony with the sounds of hard-core rock, I was quickly interested in dancing. And from there he asked me to leave with him. I guess you could see the SEX WANTED sign emblazoned on my rather ample chest. So I left with him and we went directly to my apartment. I was, let me say in a word: TERRIFIED. Apprehensive is hardly adequate for my feelings. What do I say. Where do we go? I managed to suggest that I was very thirsty even though I never touch the stuff. So he obliged and took me out for a drink and something to eat. And while he was being very seductive I couldn't get my mind off: what's next? I mean, how will he act? What do I do? If he only knew that behind the smile of desire was a stomach of acid indigestion. To bed or not to bed. This was it though. I knew it. I wanted to. Obviously. The guy rubbed my thigh and I put my hand on his knee—tentatively. And then when he smiled I withdrew like a cobra struck me. He must have thought I was crazy but he was persistent.

"Finally, after the campari soda went to my head, I sort of mentally shrugged—that's what they say in the books isn't it?—and gave in to what I wanted to do. Sleep with the man. He obviously wanted me and that was good enough for the night.

"So finally we went back to my apartment. I needed the security of my own home. Later this would change, but the first time I wanted *my* bathroom, *my* shower, *my* bed.

"We walked in and all of a sudden I became the perfect but very nervous hostess. Drink? Anything to eat? See the view? Can I hang up your coat? And then

45

I started to do the dishes left over from my breakfast. The dishes! Not very romantic, was it? But I was so nervous. And I needed time to clear my head. And what better than the retreat to the kitchen. He followed. He kissed me in the middle of soapy hands and clogged sink. We moved from there to the bedroom and carefully undressed each other. I was shaking: from his touch, from his desire, from the gut feeling of how it would feel for him to have his hands on my naked skin, let alone on my breasts or between my legs. I didn't have any more time to think: I was busy feeling.

"We moved from standing there looking at one another naked to the bed. (To be honest, I was fascinated with another man's penis.) It was obvious he liked what he saw and I must say that this was enough to get me moving and feeling and from there I didn't do much thinking. The first time we made love that night was really a time for me to be aware of his every move. I was also thinking about my movements. It was really amazing to me that before I knew it we were moving together and in response to one another. Still, I will admit that I was so aware of this newly found freedom that I did not have an orgasm. Not so the second time. My lover reached for me and you know it all seemed as if I had been making love to new men all along."

Sure, when it's a new man there are moments when you hesitate; you probe; you query his desire; you lead him to your desire. But this is a natural sensuous learning. Remember back to when you were single. Certain things haven't changed that much. And if you hadn't known other men before your husband I can assure you that the first time you sleep with a man there are always tentative moments as you are learning each other.

The chance of the first time being complete and satisfactory is rare. Candice had loved snuggling up and being comforted by a man, something she had been missing for quite some time. And that was quite enough—indeed a great deal—for the time being.

Agnes just went ahead to find out what a man felt like inside of her and didn't expect any more. And she got what she wanted.

If you believe that having an orgasm is the completed pleasure, then don't be disappointed if you don't achieve it on the eve of your first time. With all the pressures of who, what, when, and where—it's more of a miracle if you do, despite being turned on by a lover who is beyond your most salacious fantasies.

Nina is a classic example. She told me about her experience the first time:

"I found a man. There were terrific vibrations between us. I was frightened but willing to take the risk. He invited me to a party. And naturally I accepted. I kept looking at him all evening and very definitely got that tingle. And he was certainly interesting. Talk about sex in the air—you could have cut it. We left the party and went back to his place. The mood was perfect. I felt perfect. I felt gorgeous, sexy, and pretty. He was dynamite. Then the following happened. He kissed me. I responded. So far so good. He touched my breasts. I tentatively touched his cock (still unsure of myself, right?). His cock, hard. My cunt, wet. I was more sure of myself. We undressed. Now cut to: we are in bed. Foreplay, all there. Sensational. He gives. I take. I take. He gives. Whatever. The tension is excruciating—it is all pleasure. I am out of my mind. He enters and it feels gorgeous. I think of the payment due on my car. I lose. He tries. I have to say that. But I can't make it. Finally he comes and we are both disappointed. And he didn't stop trying but every time I would reach that point of falling over and letting go, I would think of something so ridiculous that it was like throwing a wet cloth on my face. I was miserable and embarrassed. I had never had that problem before. Now what? Was I destined to be one of those orgasmless women I had been reading about? I felt like I was a failure."

She soon found out that she wasn't a failure. By that weekend she was back to her old self. What happened to her was not unique. With so much going down (the pun is awful) during this time, it's not at all surprising. The solution varies for different women, as does the time it takes to completely enjoy. But don't give up and don't worry. (More on orgasm later.)

The first time may be ripe with problems but so might the first man, no matter how many times you have sex together. Dorothea's first time was with someone she really liked and cared for but they could never get it together sexually because he was the first. There were probably other reasons, but she told me: "The first fuck was the divorce decree as far as I was concerned and it was so symbolic that that's all it was: a symbol of the end of three years of marriage. Poor Johnny, my beau at the time, he never had a chance, did he?"

No, with her he didn't. The pattern had been set when they slept together the first time, and there was nothing anyone could do about that. Having once connected him with the first time and all its ramifications, she could never undo that imprint in her mind that would have freed her to enjoy sex with him.

And don't be surprised if you think of your ex— while in bed with the first. Caroline thought of her ex-husband at the point of reaching her orgasm, lost it, and thought she was ruined for life. That to her was an omen that she and her husband had been destined for each other, that they should try and make a go of it. All those thoughts despite the knowledge that it would never work—his urges to lay everything in sight seemed to be his goal in life—even on their honeymoon. But what she finally realized was something most of us do: images of ex-husbands looming in the shadows as you are making love should soon disappear. And the only thing his ghost is indicative of is: yes, you were once married to him. Nothing more.

Dana seemed to be so involved in trying to be the all-time sexual athlete her first time—and she admitted she wished her husband had been there to witness her performance. Maybe it was just as well he wasn't. All that wishing finally removed her so far from the action on hand—she never came.

NO GUILT, PLEASE

And no guilt. Please. You are no longer married.

Alice found it difficult to have orgasm her first time because she was so fascinated with the touch of a new man. Although one sense was short-circuited (climax) she had a hell of a good time, just finding out about his body . . . and made no complaints when he explored hers.

"After we got divorced, I just wandered around. My first time was neither here nor there. It was interesting because here was a whole new body after being married for four years. I had had one affair in those four years but that was the third year of my marriage. Really in the last four years I only knew one body well—my husband's. So the first time was interesting. I explored every part of his body with my hands. His skin was warmer than my husband's and it felt good. His penis was a little smaller than Donald's . . . and the funniest feeling was when we got into that old traditional position and I didn't know exactly where to put my legs. He was a lot taller than Donald . . . thinner. It was a while before I got comfortable. As a result of all this sensory perception I never did make it. I saw him for a while but somehow there was never any romance. I started seeing other guys and once I undid the memory of the familiar I no longer expected the familiar. That freed me. I never had a real problem after that."

Alice's first time may not have brought her to climax but it was essential for her to undo the old and true. After all, she was doing what came naturally.

Now that the first time is finally over and done with, it's time to take stock.

By now you should know that you still know how to do it. Hopefully, you have been reassured that a man does find you a sexual woman. If nothing else, didn't it feel good to get all that attention? And if you were really lucky, there's that yummy feeling in your stomach that there's a man out there whom you like and he likes you. And even that doesn't mean that there aren't other men out there for you to make it with.

Reactions are as varied as the women who are experiencing them. When it's all over you can expect:
- to feel desirable
- amazement that you haven't forgotten how to do it
- satisfaction sexually . . . or at least on the road toward it
- attention, all yours, to be savored
- passion—when it works

If you have gotten any of these reactions, you're on the right track. If you have had 'em all, I should say your recovery has been phenomenal. More power to you.

And if you feel nothing but disappointment? Try again. And if you feel lonely, try to remember that we've all been there.

III.

Sex With Your Ex

Breaking up is a long process. The dance of separation that leads to a final divorce (and sometimes there is even reconciliation) takes place over a long period of time. There are daily contradictions of feelings, there are attempts to be civil with each other; and there are even some people who claim they can be friends with their ex during this period (even when they are living apart) and after the divorce. Perhaps this is a peculiarly New York phenomenon, but ofter I've seen couples who have long since broken off still lunching together once a month. That this is friendship I wholly disbelieve. That it serves another purpose I am convinced. Usually it's the inability to make a clean break and face being alone so abruptly. The attempt to make it gradual often leads many to camouflage their own motives, therefore friendship is the name of the game. And yes, it is difficult to give up the relationship of someone who knows you so well—and there were good times that seem to loom now that you are no longer living together and getting on each other's nerves. It's just not so easy to break off years of being together. And if you have kids to "discuss," seeing him with some regularity is often only an excuse to see him (or vice versa).

And when all this is going on, from the time you decide to break up, then get a legal separation, then a divorce, there will be tears and laughter, conversations and discussions, lunches, dinners—and even sex.

1. It Does Happen—and for the Strangest Reasons

Having sex with your ex is an ingredient of breaking up. Curiosity about it pervades; that it happens is commonplace.

My publisher asked immediately: "Will there be anything on having sex with your husband?" Whether he may have been curious about me or he was exercising his right as publisher about the content of the book is irrelevant (and it was probably both). But he was interested.

And at least a dozen men in the last four years have asked me: Did you have sex with your husband after the divorce? (And at least half were in bed at the time—so much for taste and more on that later.)

I have found the majority of women fantasize having sex with their ex-husbands even after the papers are signed—and some women actually have—for their own very personal reasons.

"I wanted to show him what he was missing."

"I wanted to satisfy my curiosity—one last fuck."

"I wanted to be sure it was as bad as I remembered."

"I wanted to get my sex—without any problems of dating."

"I was horny and there was no one else around."

"I thought if I could get him into bed, he'd come back to me."

"I had to, he was paying the bills, wasn't he?"

"I wanted to have some fun. No harm in it."

"I wanted to show him I was cool. No hard feelings."

52

"I wanted to make sure he knew I still looked at him as a man."

"I couldn't resist his insistence."

"I just wanted to."

"It seemed like the natural thing to do."

For whatever reason, most separated couples do come together at least once during the separation periods (and maybe after the divorce) and have one last session of sex. The reasons are as complicated as the divorce. But it is part of the dance of the breaking up. And for that reason alone, no one should ever have any regrets, no one should think any less of herself. It's all part of the transition from one life to another.

Here are some stories from women with different results.

Donna was not happy about the decision to break up her two-year marriage. She thought that sex was the way back. It became an obsession with her until she finally got him into her bed.

"I guess I always lived in a make-believe world until recently. I was sure that if I could just get him into bed, everything would be all right with the world, our marriage, my life. I really believed—actually counted on him coming back, if I could just get him to spend one night with me. I wasn't being very realistic. But I was in shock. We had been married two years, never had an argument, and one day he came home and announced he wanted a divorce. We had gotten married right out of college—we had been twenty-one. From what I gathered, he just felt he shouldn't be married. That he had married too young . . . and there were lots of things he wanted to do. I pleaded, I cried, I even suggested temporary separation. But he was firm. And we got divorced. I didn't even think of fucking with another man. I spent all my time figuring a way to get him into bed—my bed—our bed. Whew. I was quite crazy. So I used my final weapon. I actually threatened to kill myself if he didn't come over that night. He came. And when he arrived I was demurely on the couch in my briefest nightie. I made the first advance. And he did get hard. I can at least

53

say that for my self-respect. And he went through the motions of making love—I should call it making hate. Because until then I don't think he hated me. But that was sure changing fast. I was making him do something that he really didn't want to. But because he felt sorry for me he was going through the motions of making love. Neither of us came. I fell asleep and when I woke up he was gone. I felt so dirty. It was a terrible idea. I was humiliated. But I know now it took that to make me realize the marriage was finished."

I think she said it all. Her inability to see that the marriage was over drove her to desperate measures. But she had no more illusions after that night.

Jackie had been married for nine years. When she and Al married there was no lack of lust. As the marriage disintegrated, it was in the bedroom that it could be seen clearly: love had turned to disinterest. It was the nature of their marriage that undid the sexual desire. That they broke up their marriage finally was the best for both of them. After the divorce, sex came into the picture once again, and for the last time.

"He and I were sorting out the books. We had been divorced for one month. It's weird. The last year of our marriage sex was a ritual to be performed as a duty—for both of us. But there I was behind a stack of books and all of a sudden I felt this rush—I wanted him. There. Now. I thought I must be going crazy. I didn't hate him but our life together was over. We both knew it. It wasn't as easy as I am making it sound but it wasn't the case of a one-sided divorce. Al was sorting books on the other side of the room. He had taken off his shirt because it was hot. He had on white Levi pants that were skin-tight. He looked up to ask me a question and caught me dead looking at his cock. And to my astonishment it was huge. He looked down at himself and up to me and when our eyes met, I shrugged and shivered. He came across the room and I nodded my head without saying a word. Right there in the library we made love for the last time. It wasn't that great but it certainly made up for the last year.

He was hard for two hours. It was like he was proving a point. But I didn't mind. So was I, I guess. When we were finished he left. When he came back to finish the book selection, I made sure I wasn't home. We never mentioned what happened. I really can't say I'm sorry. In fact, I am rather glad we had that last time. There was just something in his eye when he was on top of me that had a funny quality to it. I really can't describe it. It was like looking into the eyes of a stranger. I guess you could say that day was really the divorce. He was no longer my husband—in my mind. And so it was worth it."

Jackie needed more than a legal document to stamp the realization that she was divorced. That look in his eyes was what she needed to fully accept her new "single" status.

Judy lived in the South all her life and when she got a divorce after ten years of marriage she was hysterical. Her friends rallied and helped her put her life back together. But she rarely went out with men. Why? Because they would want sex. Questioned further, she admitted that she too wanted sex, but was afraid of what people would say. In this day and age that notion is much more prevalent than some of us realize. And the books around that pretend to advise women are so ambiguous—some outrageous and others old-fashioned —that they often are of little use. An intelligent woman, she had read a lot of these books, and we talked about her reaction. She said she was going crazy because everyone was telling her something else. I remember being impatient with her for her inability to do what she wanted. Then I looked at some of the books she was reading. A respected sexologist, Dr. LeMons, seemed to sum up this moralistic attitude that was confusing Judy when he said that sexual relations with an ex-husband are to be condoned or at least expected: "After all, she does have sexual needs regardless of our cultural or moral attitudes on the subject." The implication here is staggering. Here's a book entitled *101 Intimate Sexual Problems Answered*. And this "advisor" is almost advising the woman that her only answer for sexual outlet is with her ex if she doesn't want to be branded a terrible or immoral person. My apologies, Judy. When I pursued the subject further I found it was not uncommon to lay this trip on the divorced wife.

Maybe that's what motivated Sara:

"I was living in a small town. There were two kids and my family lived a few blocks away. I felt trapped. I also had sexual needs. So I fucked with my husband at least once a month. Only he wasn't my husband. I found that out every time he got up to leave the bed after a quick hour of sex. Well, thank God, I wasn't that sick and finally I realized there was more to sex than a quick fuck. It was hard but I finally stopped doing it. Then I had to face the cold hard facts of searching for available men to date and sleep with. And to rectify that in my head with everyone telling me about the divorcee who slept around—did they tell me those stories on purpose? Finally I realized it was my life, and if I had a boyfriend, and dated, or went on vacations there was no reason for me not to be me. But it was a long hard haul to get to the point where I didn't care what they thought."

But it was worth it. She is now remarried and living a very contented life (he, a recently divorced man with two children of his own).

Lois was lonely and discouraged. She had been married for ten years and now was faced with two kids, a big house, and an empty bed. She solved her sexual needs in a unique way that served her purpose, but. . . .

"I had been divorced for five months. I was lonely and discouraged. A lot of men had taken me out but I was afraid to go to bed. Sex with my husband was just terrific. Even up to the time he left it was good. It may be perverted but there it is; that's the truth. I guess I thought there would only be one man in the world who would make the bells ring and the bombs burst for me and he was living with his latest girl friend. Things were really getting sticky. I wanted to fuck. But I couldn't make the plunge with just anybody. So I arranged to go up to my ex-husband's office. I knew he had a big couch and a lock on the door—how convenient for him. Why shouldn't it be as convenient for me? He was cordial. I was being seductive. He did get turned on. And right there in the office, where he had been having his flings while I was home cooking for the kids, we made passionate if not lengthy love. I left feeling all's right with the world. I got what I wanted.

"Well, I did myself more harm than good. Maybe I had some dumb idea that he could service me once a month for the rest of my life. And save me the fumbling trials and errors of being with other men. I wasn't too far wrong. Every week I visited him for my weekly fix of sex. I was like a junkie. I'd start to count the days till the next time as I descended in the elevator from his office. Just in case you're thinking that I had any illusions about going back with him, I didn't. For very obvious real reasons my life with him as his wife was over. I don't know how long I would have kept up this farce if he hadn't gone on a two-month business trip. Left to my own devices, I felt I was back where I'd started. Seven months it lasted and seven months wasted as far as I'm concerned."

Taking the easy way out may have done her more damage than good. All she did was delay the long, hard pull of re-entry into the world as an independent woman who could make it on her own.

One woman was so in need of sex and there seemed to be no one around who could arouse her so she tracked down her ex and got him into bed. Her reasons:

"It was a known quantity. I knew he could excite me. I knew what was expected of me. I knew (or thought) I would have an orgasm. It was comfortable and I knew what to expect. And when I got him there, it was all those things. But I had to face that the relationship wasn't. But at least I got fucked. I even fantasized we'd go back. And then when the fucking was over we reverted back to old habits and started arguing and then that was that. He left my place. And I still wanted to fuck with him again and did a few times. Finally, I found someone who could turn me on and that was the end of my longing for my ex-husband."

It worked for her. At least she didn't feel that she was regressing or doing anything unhealthy. She knew what she needed and wanted, and got it. If it was using him, so be it. Sex wasn't a one-way street. He was getting his, wasn't he?

Jennifer thought it would be fun to seduce her ex-husband. She invited him over to the house on the pretext of clearing out the basement (it was mostly his skiing equipment). She had no intentions of patching up the separation. She did give in to her loneliness, and called it "having a little fun." But she didn't expect his reaction.

"I thought it would be fun to have sex with my ex. For old time's sake. But he didn't see it that way. He thought it was tantamount to saying I would be his wife again. What a drag. It was all my fault but I never thought he'd take my suggestion to spend the night as anything but that. He almost moved in. It was an awful moment. He did spend the night and it was fun for both of us. We had been drinking and this dulled all reality thoughts. We just concentrated on doing things to each other that we remembered we liked from the first months of our marriage. He sucked my toes; I licked his nipples; I tickled his cock with a feather; he played with my breasts like he was milking a cow; and then he went inside of me from behind—our most exciting position together. Then we fell asleep very very satisfied. I never once thought he thought all was forgiven. Certain things hadn't changed: he still didn't work (he had a small income to live on and it prevented him from ever taking a real job) and he still managed to drink four martinis in an evening. He was still self-centered, arrogant, and cruel. And he could still turn me on. But I didn't want to make a life with him. So the next morning he got up before I did and said he was going to call the club and tell them he was moving out. In perfect innocence I asked where. Then the explosion from him and the cruel side: 'Here, you cunt,' he shouted. 'Where I can have that sweet pussy any time I want it, day or night.' It was like old times. The abuse was awful. But I guess I deserved it. I was really a shit. My advice to any woman who wants to seduce her ex would be to make damn well sure he isn't going to take it as an invitation to reconciliation."

Jennifer should have known better. Toying with her husband's feelings was cruel even if he was abusive. At least it was the last time.

Don't you make the mistake that sleeping with your ex means anything more than what it is. Georgia and Tom are typical. They had split up after eleven years of marriage. She told me that he came over every Sunday to take the kids out (aged ten and seven). Usually he'd drop them off but one day he seemed to hang around. She invited him for a cup of coffee and as they say in the soaps, it was only the first step. . . .

"He had agreed to the divorce. And we both were trying to pull our lives into shape. One afternoon he stopped by the house to see the kids. We were sitting at the kitchen table talking. He couldn't have been there more than five minutes when he reached over, took my head, and pulled my face toward his. It just seemed natural. And probably for the same reason I didn't resist when he led me into our—no, my—bedroom. I really don't think he had it in his mind when he came over and I certainly didn't when I asked if he wanted a cup of coffee. I was very upset when he got up to leave. I guess I thought if he wanted sex, he'd want to stay married. My mistake, and it hurt."

She had no idea what Tom had in his mind when he reached for her but he made it quite clear it was a momentary desire. Georgia had a few hours of thinking that the marriage could begin again. Prolonging the agony is what that's called.

No one has a sense of the drama like my friend

Amanda. But she knew what she was doing. She had never had trouble having orgasms when she was married, but suddenly she couldn't come with the man she had been seeing since the separation. She was overwhelmed by the idea that maybe her husband was the only man in the world she could ever have an orgasm with. So she decided to see what that was all about.

"Okay. If you ask a straight question, I'll answer it. Yes, I did have one last fling with my husband . . . when he was no longer my husband. Frankly it was the right thing to do. After the divorce I was that fair game you talk about. And I had the sense to take advantage of it. But it seemed like it was getting me nowhere. No matter whom I chose to sleep with, I just couldn't make it. This was wrong, that was wrong. I was super critical. See, I knew I could come. I always did with my husband. So I started feeling sorry for myself. And I had all kinds of misgivings. Maybe I should have tried to make a go of it. I mean, maybe things weren't so bad being married. Four months had gone by. And when I look back I realize that's a very short time but then it seemed like an age. In my mind what had been fairly good sex became the be-all and end-all of ecstasy. And the more I thought that way, the less chance I had of any men getting to me. So when my husband—he had come over to finish the job of moving his things—reached for me I responded. We fucked with more enthusiasm than two kids in their first bed. He couldn't have been more attentive, sexual, and giving. And the damndest thing happened— or didn't happen—depending on how you look at it. I couldn't come. It was the first time that ever happened with him. That was food for thought. Something told me it was me who just wouldn't lose control to any man. So I took myself to a therapist and changed my attitude toward the man I was dating. It worked. In three weeks exactly, I had my first orgasm since my divorce. And if I hadn't had sex with my husband I don't think my recovery would have been that simple."

Some women start to get dreamy-eyed about their ex-husband—that same man whom they would have gladly fed to the lions not six months before. Sometimes it's worth a night to get rid of that fantasy once and for all. Thea did:

"Simply put, I really had it all wrong. I managed to remember only the great sex with my husband. I have been divorced three years now and have remarried, so I have some perspective. It wasn't all that good. But the more men I slept with right after the divorce, the better my ex-husband seemed to get. The fuzzy memory was set back into focus. I maneuvered my husband into a situation where he couldn't fail to respond to my seduction. Christ, what a night. It just wasn't as good as I remembered it. I am grateful I had a chance to get rid of the blurs. In fact, it was quite ordinary. We had established a set pattern and routine. Something like: he undresses me; I undress him. I hold his balls; he sucks my pussy. I lick his cock; he pinches my tits. Then I get on top of him and come home. Then his turn. All very tried and true. No variation. And hardly what one would call lovemaking. No passion. I had been with enough men since the divorce to know that something was missing—spontaneity, something. I think he felt the same way. We had outgrown each other. And unfortunately for us we couldn't break out of the pattern together. We had to do it with other partners. There's probably something neurotic about the whole thing. But really I have no regrets. I did the right thing for me—looked at the men around me with a whole new eagerness. And began to treat every new sexual experience as a treat. And I would even venture to say that it worked the same way for my husband. Yes, it was the right thing to do for both of us."

I would agree. Yes, it was the right thing. Do you agree?

And here are two more views to add. Somehow these two women were surprised that I even asked the question: "Did you have sex with your ex-husband after you agreed to separate?" Here are their answers:

"My husband was a sex maniac, is all. And he was still turned on by me even though he was busy satisfying three other women. When he made a pass, I went along. We had sex and he left. That was it. Next time he tried I was in the midst of developing a lovely relationship with a man who knew thirty-two different positions of coitus. So I said no. And there were no hard feelings. I don't see where fucking him that time was bad. I can see if it got to be a habit where it could really mess you up, but once is no hassle."

"The day the divorce was final, my husband and I went to dinner. And as if we both had planned it, we came home and fucked all night. It was a very fitting way to celebrate the divorce. I mean, it wouldn't be appropriate with anyone else, would it?"

Self-esteem is worth fighting for. And often the divorced wife has the hardest battle to win. And each woman must determine what her battle is and fight like hell. Nancy was rather precise when I asked her about sex with her ex.

"I had been with four different men since the divorce and I really never enjoyed it. Well, without going into it, I concocted this elaborate plan to get my ex into bed with me. I was that desperate. Hah. I would have been better off picking up someone at a bar. But who knows? The odds were on my side this time. I thought. But I was so fucked up at that time that I wanted to see if it really was as bad as I remembered it. Some rationalization. It just couldn't be as bad as the creeps in my life. You see, the husband was impotent at the time. I have to call him the husband . . . I just can't think in terms of *my* husband. Anyway that's not the point, is it? Not only was he impotent. But he blamed *me*. Me for his inadequacy. And I'm so stupid half the time when it comes to men . . . I bought it. The whole thing. I really had a lousy view of myself and if anything went wrong anywhere I figured it was because I fucked it up. I was the fuck up of all time.

It just never occurred to me that someone else can fuck up. So there I was Mrs. Fuck Up of the sixties. Then I advanced in my thinking. I woke up. It wasn't just my problem. It was *our* problem. Togetherness all the way. Well, it was my problem to the extent that I had to sleep with the guy. Anyway. I would have done anything to keep the marriage together and to make him happy. That's what made me happy . . . to make him happy. So I tried to get him into some kind of counseling with me. He was furious. He was adamant that if anyone needed therapy it was me because I was crazy and perverted and nuts . . . blah, blah, blah . . . the typical reaction. I was to blame. It was my fault that he couldn't keep an erection. And that was that. He closed the subject. Making love—that's a misnomer —was a trial. It always ended in tears, accusations, an argument, bad feelings, and frustration. But there I was, willing to subject myself to this mess because the men in my life were so awful. I just forgot how awful my husband was. He was looking better and better. This was about five months after the divorce. What was really bothering me was, maybe he was right. Maybe I was as bad as he said.

"Anyway, ready to take on the full blame for all that went wrong, I enticed him into my bed. The details of how are really unnecessary. We undressed; I caressed his cock for hours. I licked it and sucked it; I pulled and pushed; I caressed fast, slow, quickly, gently, you name it, I did it. It got very very hard and I got very very wet. I was getting turned on just working on him. Needless to say he didn't do much to aid that. Then, when it came time for me to get him into my very ready, very wet pussy, he went limp as sauerkraut. Shit, was I pissed. Fuck up did it again. But he was pissed too. Nothing had changed. He left finally, not without having the last word: 'You're still a lousy lay.' That set me back months in my self-esteem— what there was of it. And then I went into a real depression. Which, when I look back, was probably the best thing that ever happened. Because that got me to a shrink. And now that I have had a year of therapy,

I realize that I am worthy. I give and I can also be worth someone giving to me. And I'm not so quick to make sure he is satisfied. I am worth some attention from him. And slowly my own regard has built up and now I am attracting men who at least give and take. And you know . . . I learned something. Sex is great. Hard work. But great. And actually if I hadn't had such a lousy experience with the husband I probably would still be going from man to man . . . ready to administer to their needs, be unsatisfied, and the whole thing would be going on. But that lousy-lay business with the ex was so devastating that I knew I needed professional help. Sense of survival. And, knock wood, I'm not saying I'm still not fucked up in lots of ways but at least I'm having a better time about it."

Many women I talked to told me that they never would have had sex with their ex husbands, although no woman said it was out of the question or that she never entertained the thought. Some failed to get him into the bed even if they tried; others said no when he tried and then got indignant. I say, do what you want. Have no regrets. It, after all, is only a moment in time, and it may be just what you need to finalize the divorce.

2. Don't Discuss Your Sex Life With Your Ex

A funny thing happens when you separate or divorce. The legal document says you are no longer man and wife. Yet your ex may, so many men do, still feel that you are his wife (and you may still feel married to him). But usually the bond is out of phase. Your ex may feel that you are still his sexual property; even if the sight of you makes his blood turn cold, the idea of you in bed with another man would make his blood churn. In other words, his ego is at stake. No matter what he says, there are usually signs of this dog-in-the-manger attitude. The woman, on the other hand, often sees her man as someone who should care if she is ill, unhappy, or broke—and sometimes he is still

64

paying her bills, especially if there are children. A generalization to be sure, but the point is, rarely does she see her husband—or by now ex—as her own private sexual property. There are no surprises when she finds out with whom he is involved in a sexual relationship. It is to be expected. That this is the imprint of conditioning of the famous double standard and the traditional male-female and/or husband-wife roles cannot be disputed. That it is changing is obviously true. That you don't know where your ex is in his development of that "generation of thought" is what this chapter is all about. And absolutely no purpose is served by letting him in on where you head is at (or has been!).

The topic of sex should be forbidden between ex-husband and ex-wife. One divorced wife told me she wanted to tell her ex about her lovers who found her a "great piece of ass" just to show him that he had been wrong: their bad sex life wasn't her fault. Another woman told me that her husband blamed their breakup on her own lack of enthusiasm in bed. That he was in fact a selfish lover was more to the point. But she didn't know that until months later, after having experienced a variety of men. And then she told me she wanted to let him in on that little fact. Swallowing the urge, she was relieved because when it came time to actually sign the papers she felt it was no longer any of his business where she was sleeping. And she was right. Another woman wasn't so lucky: she told her husband about her new sex life and was staggered when it came out in the judge's chambers as the papers were being signed. When it came to her settlement of alimony, there was none. The laws of her state and the feelings of the court were that her sex life made her unworthy. That the laws are unworthy is not the point. That your sex life is still being controlled by laws *is*. So keep it to yourself. Which leads me to the next point: The law is on your husband's side when it comes to your bedroom. Ask your lawyer, today:

If you are no longer living together and not yet legally separated, what are your sexual rights?

If you are no longer living together, but have filed legal separation papers, what are your sexual rights?

If you are no longer living together and have a final divorce decree, what are your sexual rights? Especially if you have children.

When I asked one woman what she felt her husband thought of her sex life after her divorce, she started to laugh. She could laugh because the divorce had taken place over four years ago. She hadn't been laughing then. She had been having an affair while married and finally decided to leave her husband and move in with her lover. Her husband was faced with the facts and the break took place. He shouldn't have been in for any more surprises, but he was. He just couldn't accept that any man could be a better lover to his wife than he had been. One day as they were discussing the settlement he said to her: I never thought you would give up a great sex life like we had for a million dollars." Her new paramour was wealthy, and her husband preferred to think that that was the reason she was leaving him, never once facing the fact that their sex-life passion had died months before her affair ever started.

Most women do have some fantasies about letting their ex know that some men find them desirable—even if he didn't. I would have liked to have sent my ex a dozen roses for every orgasm I had for the first six months after our separation. That I didn't was due more to my financial status at the time than anything else. And that of course worked to my advantage. There would have been no predicting what he would have done with that information (and he would probably have given the roses to his new girl friend). That's my whole point—no matter what the circumstances of your split, there is no predicting your ex-husband's reaction to finding out that you are having sex with anyone; that it may be great; that it may be terrible; that it may even be better than he was. (And that there may be a series of lovers would blow the fuse altogether, wouldn't it?)

You may be giving him hope you'll be back together; you may be discouraging a reconciliation (and that is a possibility); you may infuriate him to the point of becoming unreasonable when it comes to settling things; it may be totally disastrous.

And if you manage to repress the urge to send telegrams announcing your new sex life, make sure you aren't leaving any hints around to imply the same. If you have children, obviously your husband will be around; if you are breaking up an apartment or household, he also will be paying some visits. Don't leave any incriminating—male-type—evidence around for him to connect with your passionate lovemaking last weekend.

Sandra agreed with this fully. She was well aware of the possibilities of leaving tell tale signs around the apartment: shaving lotion, a jacket, even shoes.

"I see no reason to let my ex in on my personal life. After we separated, he'd come over and we'd have our 'discussions' about what went wrong. You know the thing. It's inevitable. And before his arrival I made damned sure that one of my latest lovers hadn't left anything around that would have indicated intimacy. Even another brand of cigarettes. My husband was so nutsy he could see things even where there weren't and since I wasn't exactly living a celibate life . . . well, I decided to keep him out of it. I even made sure the medicine chest didn't have anything 'male' in it. I don't know about you, but often I open a medicine chest in a friend's place to find an aspirin and sometimes even to satisfy curiosity. If I've done it just out of curiosity, who's to say my ex wouldn't do it? And even if it wasn't a question of his getting some kind of revenge. We didn't have that kind of relationship. I just didn't want to take the chance. Furthermore, I felt that he might start talking to me about his affairs. And that I wasn't up to at all."

Another woman had a bad scare by her own carelessness:

"I had a horrible scare. My kids were at camp. I

was divorced two months. And maybe I did a terrible thing. But I did it. I spent the entire weekend in bed at my house with a guy I had been seeing for a few weeks. It was such a luxury with the kids away. And I felt I deserved it. My husband meanwhile was being really peculiar about the custody of the kids. He really could use them against me. And his mother was making all kinds of noises about his rights as a father. You know—spend time with him and with me. She wanted them for the summer. But they always went to camp. The oldest one for the last five years. To interrupt their schedule would have been a perfectly dreadful thing to do. They had enough to cope with when we got divorced. Anyway, my husband came over to collect more of his stuff. Since I had the house and he had moved into an apartment, I was keeping his things for him. It's the least I could do. Anyway, he wanted his camping equipment. And in the shed he found a pair of sneakers. I don't really know how they got there but I did know the last person to be in the shed was my lover. We had gone sailing and he had put away the sail and a bunch of other stuff. Joe came back into house dangling the sneakers with 'Whose' written all over his smug face. How could I tell him they belonged to cousin Herbert, who had stayed a week? After all, my husband knew that I loathed cousin Herbert. Sometimes nothing is better than anything. So I said nothing. He dropped the sneakers on the couch and didn't say another word about it. But he sure had me scared. Now I make damned sure there is no evidence around for him to gloat over or use against me. And since he sees the kids once a week, I do a double check every time he comes to pay his respects. I have to be cautious now. After a time I don't think he'll be so uptight. And he'll stop hating me and he'll realize his mother really can't take the kids for him."

This was a close call. Don't ever give anyone ammunition to call you an unfit mother. That you should be a mother of three children, working to support them, divorced, and want a regular sex life is only normal. But "regular sex life" somehow is open to interpretation: your husband's, yours, and the courts. The laws must have been made by men who saw the mother of their children as virginal to all men except themselves. It seems they have spent a lot of energy trying to keep you from fulfilling your needs—sex included. It doesn't mean you should abstain but it does behoove you to exercise a little caution. You have something at stake, fair or no, and flaunting your sex life or carelessness about it can lead to disaster and unwanted aggravation.

If you discuss your sex life with your ex-husband you may be opening up a whole guilt trip. One woman rues the day she hinted at hers to her ex:

"I had to open my big mouth. I was having lunch with my ex to discuss selling our summer house. I don't know exactly what I said, but it somehow came out that I was getting all the sex I wanted. It was insignificant to me but huge tears welled up in his eyes. He said: 'I hope you're happy.' He had had a few drinks and tended to get blurry-eyed and maudlin when he drank. 'Since you left, I can't bear to touch another woman. I can't even get it up.' Then he proceeded to lay this whole trip on me. I certainly had no intention of going back but I really felt sorry for him. I took no pleasure in hearing about his impotence. But I certainly wasn't going to personally do anything about it. From then on I went out of my way to avoid the word sex and in fact, shortly after, those lunches stopped."

She learned her lesson and in addition learned what those lunches were all about. He had hoped he could get to her, and that they would get back together if he could make her feel sorry for him. Thank God it didn't work. But it was an unnecessary scene to have to play out.

And even if you have agreed after your separation that you both should be dating, don't be surprised when he shows up at your place while the two of you are taking a shower together. "No strings attached" somehow never seems to have any application when it comes to the bedroom. So if it's freedom you are being given, guard it well. And don't make unnecessary complications by blabbing about your new life to your ex (or soon-to-be ex).

Don't be fooled when your ex shows interest . . . even if he says it's in your best interest. If you let down your guard and confide in him there is no predicting the response. This one was unique but I think other women can relate to it:

"I was sitting with my ex about six weeks after the separation. We were deciding about the divorce and we both knew that it was the only way to do it before we started to kill each other. We still had some good feelings between us and had been married for about six years. Our lives, however, just didn't mesh anymore and divorce was the only answer. It wasn't easy but we were doing it. At one point he said to me: 'I understand if you have to sleep with other men.' I couldn't believe my ears. *He understands.* It was so typical of him and at the same time I was surprised. Who the hell was he to *understand?* As if I were doing something *wrong.* As if he had anything to say about it anyway!"

Male patronizing no longer surprises me. Sympathy is sometimes much more a function of his own ego than the facts indicate. That he is trying to *understand* clearly indicates that he thinks that her sleeping with anyone but him was wrong. And because he cares he will tolerate or condone her *terrible* behavior. Be alert for this kind of understanding. It could be calculated to make you feel like you are still his property (you aren't) or you are "dirty" (and you're not).

Often a woman feels that she is "no good" if she is sleeping with a variety of men (that's what her mother and father taught her, isn't it?). And there are no doubt moments when she does blame her husband—ex-husband—for this feeling. It's much easier to say "he made me do it," than "I did it myself because I wanted to" (nice girls don't want to); or "I couldn't stand the loneliness one minute longer" (what, and admit to that?). In either case, it's part of the growing-up process: these inner feelings of self-contempt. They go away usually. But don't make the mistake of telling your ex about them. He may react like Sylvia's husband and "understand" and in doing that be so damning that the end result is a bad headache and a long cry. On the other hand, hasn't he been blamed for enough? And aren't you willing to take responsibility for your own actions? And it's none of his goddamned business anyway.

And don't do as Gloria did—say yes because of some kind of misplaced obligation. She and her husband had been married for eleven years before they got divorced. He agreed to a generous settlement for her (she hadn't worked in those years) and also child support. But he wanted to be paid back in sex.

"I thought we had handled ourselves so well during the whole damned mess. We were both anxious to do the best for the kids and we knew that if we stayed married our psychologies were so opposite that we would wind up hating each other and destroying ourselves more and the kids also. So it was settled and to make a long story short, one weekend he came to the six-year-old's birthday party, one of those with adults and kids present; he had a few drinks. But everyone was in a good mood. Then he helped me clean up after everyone left, and the kids were so tired they were glad to go to bed early. Then he had another drink and then the surprise: attack. I pushed him away and then he started up all over again. I had no desire to sleep with him, fuck him, or kiss him. But he was insistent. He then said something that made me hate him forever: 'As long as I'm paying the bills around here, I'm entitled to fuck you.' He had me terrified. I really didn't thing he could undo the agreement but I was just too worried about it to find out. So I said yes that night and hated every minute of it. The next day I saw my lawyer, who assured me that it wasn't in his rights. And the next time he tried, I was firm. I hate myself for saying yes the first time, but I just didn't know what to do."

There is always the threat that he will withdraw

emotional and financial support, but try not to get sucked in on that ploy. Saying yes to him when no is the answer will just delay your progress in feeling one hundred percent yourself again.

IV.

If You Have Kids,
You Have Special Problems

If you keep your sense of humor and do some careful planning, you should be able to function as a woman—with kids. I have no children so I relied on two sources to find out how it's done.

First, a number of women who were willing to talk to me provided a great deal of material for the entire book. They also brought up a number of points that I feel should be included in a separate—this—chapter. Some of these women I knew for years, others I found through mutual friends. In both cases, we didn't need long, formal interview questions. Rather, we talked and laughed (problems must have their humorous side in order to solve them). All of the women knew I was doing this book and wanted very much to share their experiences with me. The few who were uptight about talking about sex would have been even if they didn't have children. And only one refused to talk to me on the grounds that I had no children and didn't understand her problems.

It isn't easy to re-enter the world as a divorced woman and it is even more difficult when you have children. Motherhood has been looked upon as a virginal state, biology notwithstanding. But that is the image men have fostered about women for centuries and written into the laws we have to face today. It influences our thinking as well as limits our behavior. Women, as well, have been guilty of going all out to preserve that image; if not that, then to adhere to the common attitudes of others. Meanwhile the divorced woman is faced with questions that boggle the mind: What will my kids think if they see me with a man who is not their father? How will it look if I go away for the weekend with a man and leave my kids with their grandparents? Am I an unfit mother if I enjoy the attentions of men and occasionally enjoy sex with them?

Obviously there is no single answer for everyone. Each woman has to work it out for herself. Trying to do right by her children and fulfilling her sexual needs often are the most trying aspect of adjusting to divorce. And always the woman should be aware of the laws of her state regarding her behavior and her ex-husband's acceptance of her as a woman with sexual needs. For that, don't take the advice of a friend; go see a lawyer.

Otherwise, working it out is up to you. Even the most liberated woman finds it difficult to reconcile her normal natural needs with the needs of her children. Even in today's novels, confusion and hypocrisy is apparent. Dorothy Monet in *Squandering* writes about a divorced woman living in New York, an independent woman with a career who manages to survive, still worries about the effect her social/sexual life might have on her child.

"A single woman living with a child in New York might just as well be living in the YWCA. Running in and out of the Stanhope Hotel to be with David at unearthly hours all the bitter New York winter had been a mother's sacrifice rarely credited to motherhood, and hardly one I could throw up to Carla when she was being particularly ungrateful. Not even on

74

Mother's Day . . . Carla is a flower child and way far out as far as anybody else's sex life is concerned, but where I'm concerned, I'm the Holy Virgin Mother and she's the virgin birth."

Fact often imitates fiction. One woman, an editor with a large national women's magazine, openly and candidly admitted her hypocritical stance about her sex life when it came to her kids:

"I love sex but when it comes to my kids (Tommy, aged five, and Cynthia, aged seven) I am the Virgin Mary. I'll talk to you but warn you I am a hypocrite. I advocate one thing and act another. I know it's wrong but I can't seem to get affectionate with any man in front of the kids. And I manage to fulfill my sexual needs when the kids are not around. If I am sleeping with a guy, it's at his place. And then I make sure I am home in time for the kids when they wake up in the morning. I may be the most passionate of all lovers for a few hours, but then I am up and out and return home with every hair in place. I may have had four orgasms in four different positions but when I arrive home, as far as anyone is concerned, I don't even know the meaning of kissing."

She still insists this is the only way for her to reconcile her needs. As long as she gets what she wants, who am I to say different? At least she's not sitting at home. However, she is paying a price for the deception.

Other women face the facts and come to terms with the role of mother and "woman. Madge has:

"Sex just comes naturally. I don't see where having a normal sex life is any different or more difficult for me than it would be for someone without children—for you, for example. My kids know that I like men who are not their father. They are eight and ten and seem to adjust very well to the men in my life. It's more normal for them, I think, than being with me all the time. Their father comes to visit once a week and then they are left without a man. The men in my life provide that masculine—if you will—atmosphere that would be lacking. My affection for both the kids and the man are an extension of me. And when the man in my life spends the night it's only natural. I don't do it that often and when I do it's with someone the kids have grown accustomed to seeing at dinner, around the house. When he appears at breakfast they don't seem to see any difference than when he appears at dinner. And why should they, if we don't make a big deal about it?"

Some women hold back on their natural instincts because they are afraid of what people might think. More concerned about others than herself, Molly was in a turmoil about what she should do. Married five years when she and her husband split, she was left with two children to support. A short, dark-haired, creamy-skinned thirty-one-year-old, she had no trouble attracting men. But once she did she was paralyzed with indecision.

"I couldn't believe it. When my friends got divorced, and there were at least three couples within two years, we sat around and discussed if their kids were getting enough care. And two of those three women started fairly active social lives and we were scandalized. And I hate to admit it but I was one of those women who was doing the jealous-biddie routine. Oh, yes, I say jealous because I realize now that we were all jealous that these women were rid of the daily routine, going out, and living it up—we thought. We had to say terrible things or we couldn't justify why we were living such drab and miserable lives. And our husbands were just as bad: just jealous that they weren't the suitors, probably. Or maybe they were afraid one of us would be next. And I know my husband, he may have hated my guts but he never wanted to see me in bed with another guy. Then it hit me. Dave and I were divorced last year. With two kids, both in nursery school. I was scared to look at any man, married or unmarried. What would my friends say? And then it got kind of lonely. And then fortunately for me one of the women who was divorced called me and invited me and my kids over for dinner. It changed my whole attitude. I realized I was on the outside looking in. She

76

was there with one of her beaus who was creating the latest scandal at the bridge club. He had been seen leaving her house after spending the night there. But I met him and I realized that he really was a part of the family. I talked to her about it later in the week and she was surprisingly candid. I asked her if she wasn't afraid of what the neighbors would think . . . some such nonsense: she really put me in my place. She said to me: 'No matter where you are and what you do there is going to be talk. And what I do and what you'll have to do is ignore it. I make sure my behavior is proper for me and for my kids, that I am providing a stable, warm home for them, and that's it. I am not a virgin. And the biological me is not expected to be celibate. I am a woman with needs. So are you. I suggest you look at them. Cope with them. Fill them. And then you can begin being a woman.' "

Molly is typical of far too many women who are unsure of themselves and are afraid to assert themselves. Fortunately, she had a friend to set her straight. Do you need one?

Some women really believe that they have no rights.
I was appalled when I heard one woman express herself: "I have no right to want to date or sleep with a man. I am a mother. A good mother."

Ester was taught: A mother's place is with her children. And she worked hard to be super mother. No time for herself began to take its toll.

"I was always afraid to date, let alone sleep with a man, because I thought my responsibility was to be home every night with the kids. I was getting grouchier and grouchier. Facing the world with my kids. I began to date finally when I met this guy who was from out of town and married. Somehow that suited my needs. He came into town regularly and I had dinner with him and stayed a few hours at his hotel, then home to the kids. I realized that I was a much more even-tempered mother and that I would have to make the effort to socialize even more. That relationship made me accept the notion that I needed men, a social life, and a sex life . . . in order to be a better mother."

Ester came to terms with her own sexuality, and her married lover was very convenient. Although it had its built-in limitations—no accident that—she realized her children had not suffered by her taking an evening for herself.

Some divorced women were reluctant to talk to me because they felt I had it easy when it came to my re-entry. They felt that I wouldn't understand their problems, and that I didn't have any problems. One woman, Gladys, admitted she felt that way about her good friend Carol. Both had been divorced. Carol had no children. Gladys had two. She found out, in a dramatic way, that both were bruised by divorce, both had different problems, but having children could be solace for loneliness.

"I was really jealous of my friends who were divorced and hadn't had any children. I thought they had it so easy. And I blamed my kids for the longest time for not allowing me to have what I considered a normal life. I didn't make any effort to go out or to date. I just assumed that I couldn't do that until they were both tucked safely away at school and since they were ten and twelve years old, that was at least eight years away. Terrific. I was making all the proper sacrifices and not only was I hating my divorced friends who were going out, but I was beginning to hate my kids. And then I would hate myself for hating them. I was getting really edgy and crazy. I felt life had played me a dirty trick—one day. And then the next day I would be glad that I had the kids to share my life with. I just couldn't be consistent. And I was running hot and cold. This wasn't a case of ups and downs; it was a case of dramatic highs and lows. Then it was Thanksgiving and I decided to have dinner as usual. It was tradition. And I invited everyone who seemed to be stray, with no plans for the holiday. At that time I had a particularly good friend who had just recently been divorced after three years of marriage. We didn't talk about it too much because, frankly, I knew she was seeing a lot of men and I was jealous. I almost didn't invite her for Thanksgiving; I figured she'd be with one of her lovers.

"But I did invite her and she accepted and it was settled. I also had my son's friend and his mother—she was divorced; and a couple I knew with no children; and a guy I know who was depressed because he too was divorced and he rarely saw his kids. It really was a motley crew. But I got the kids together and we planned Thanksgiving dinner. Ten and twelve are terrific ages because the kids could enjoy their responsibilities. The weekend before Thanksgiving was great fun as we shopped together and fixed up the house and planned the menu. Then Thursday—and the night before, Wednesday—we all worked very hard setting the table and preparing the desserts. The turkey was served to twelve people and was a great success. And Carol, my friend, burst into tears about the time Cary served her chocolate chip cookies with the pumpkin pie. Cary was ten—she had made the cookies herself, just for the first time. Carol just ran from the room as if a bolt had hit her. I followed her into my bedroom, where she was crying. She said to me: 'You're so lucky you can share Thanksgiving with Cary and Carl; they love you. And you all are having so much fun and there is so much love.' It just hit me, then and there, that I had some things that she didn't have. Since I had guests I couldn't pursue the conversation and Carol pulled herself together and faced the group with honesty: 'All this love just made me feel how lonely I am.' And then she smiled and we all hugged her and the warmth in the room was wonderful.

"The next day, with the leftovers all over the kitchen and the kids at their friends', I called Carol. She had gotten me thinking. She wasn't so lucky. I had things she didn't have. I had the warmth of never being alone. Although lonely, there were pleasures to give and to take from my children. I realized she wasn't luckier, she was just different. Once I stopped thinking that the kids were interfering with my social life I realized that all it took was some extra effort and careful planning and I could also be going out. Maybe not as much as Carol, and maybe with less spontaneity, but I certainly didn't have to be home, alone, always."

It's not necessarily easier for a woman with children to come and go as she pleases. I'm not trying to say that. I am trying to tell you there are some joys with children that a childless divorced woman doesn't have: the warmth of your daughter as she brings you her latest drawing from school; when you tuck the kids into bed; when your son finally gets that car of his into mint condition.

No matter how old or young the kids, they are a life-giving force for you. And although you might cry out for some time to yourself, remember you are not alone.

Don't fall into the trap of thinking that your life would be that different if you didn't have kids. It's self-defeating. "If I hadn't had the kids I would be free," I heard from one divorced woman with three young children. She had gotten married in her twenties, stayed married for twelve years, and her kids were nine and ten. She was thirty-five years old, attractive, and had continued her career during her marriage. But when it came time to face the divorce she felt trapped by her kids. When I heard her say she'd be free, I asked her: Free to do what? "Free to live the way I want, to go where I want, date the men I want, travel when I want, and sleep when and with whom I want," she replied. I suggested that that was pure fantasy on her part, no one had that kind of freedom.

Sometimes, when the children are older, women have difficulty in facing their offspring with their naturally needy self. Charlotte had always been the all-knowing, well-meaning, self-possessed mother, but when it came time to admit to her kids that she was also a woman with needs, she was embarrassed.

"I couldn't face the kids with the fact that I needed a social life. Then one day my daughter, Elizabeth, sat me down and gave me the facts of life. She was sixteen at the time. I had been married eighteen years when the divorce became final. I was only forty years old and I felt like a hundred. I was in pretty good shape but somehow I just couldn't see myself in bed with a man. What would my daughter think if I announced I was going away for a weekend with a man? Well this conversation cleared the air. It started with her polite inquiry about my social life. I answered as noncommittally as possible. But I wasn't prepared for her direct attack: 'Mother, have you slept with a man since Daddy and you got divorced?' I couldn't believe it. My daughter asking me that question. It made me realize two things: One, I was uptight about dating because it would most likely have led to that question. And two, I was really uptight about sex itself, not really knowing what to do or think.

"We had a long conversation, mostly her telling me it wasn't normal for me not to be going out and having sex with men. When I got over the shock of my 'baby' being that grown-up and matter-of-fact about my sex life, I began to think about what she had to say. She wasn't holding me back; I was holding myself back. I was scared for me; and I had been using her. Things changed after that."

She was ignoring some real problems by hiding behind her responsibilities as a mother. She was afraid of the hard work it would take to get back into the swing of things and blamed her lack of freedom for not facing what she could do to make her life fulfilling.

Other women ignore their appearance, eliminate any kind of social life, refuse dates, and use the children as an excuse. "I don't have the time. What would my kid think if I left him with the babysitter one night?" That's ridiculous. All kids have to learn to be with a babysitter; if you were married, you would have left the kids behind for an evening out. It's not any different now.

Make sure you aren't overdoing it, however. Children are very needy and require extra assurances from you after their father leaves the house. Don't forget that

81

the kids are there and you have to help them cope with their new situation.

"I realized I was having a little bit too much action at my place when my four-year-old daughter looked at my date and said: 'Are you going to stay overnight too?' I felt awful and embarrassed and I realized that I was not only doing awful things to myself, but I would have to consider my daughter's bewilderment. I just didn't think she was that aware for four years old. I cried and cried and cried all night after my date left. I really had only spent the night at home with two men in the eight months I had been divorced. But my daughter remembered. I had some real problems. I went to a family-type therapist who suggested some child counsel as well as therapy for me. Thank God she said it. Now I realize that she needs more security before I can bring men around and be affectionate with them."

Once you get out on the date, don't use the kids to turn him off. No matter how nice a guy he is, he'll have to get tired to continual conversation about your children.

"I messed up the most interesting relationship that had come along in months by talking about my kids all the time. I was careful enough not to talk about my ex-husband but I really laid it on about the kids. I was defensive about being a good mother, I guess. I figured if the guy wanted me, he'd have to take the kids too. But there's a time and place for everything, I learned. No man wants to talk about baby pictures when he has gone to the trouble of making a very, very special evening for you."

Often the only time a divorced woman can fully relax is on a trip by herself. If you can get away, it's terrific for the ego.

"My kids went to visit their father for two weeks and I decided to take a holiday. And get laid. It was really quite calculating on my part. I saved my money and since it was off-season got a great package deal and went to Puerto Rico for the weekend. My mother

82

was really upset; she didn't think it was *right* for me to go alone. But it was very, very right for me to go alone. That was the whole plan. I was scared shitless but I went. And spotted a marvelous-looking man at the roulette the first night I was there. And the next day at the pool I said hello. And that night at dinner I smiled. And that night at the roulette table, we laughed together and then I went to bed alone—intentionally. I said before and I'll say again I've never been so calculating. On the fourth night, I said yes. And for the rest of the holiday. It was dreamy and marvelous and I came home feeling awfully good. It was the first time since my divorce that I had had sex and after that I wasn't so on edge, you know, looking, wondering, etc. Everything became natural after that . . . so to speak."

Getting away from the routine and taking your kids often helps to establish a new life for you and paves the road to re-entry. If you plan it right, it can serve your needs as well as the kids'. *And summer plans can more than likely serve the purpose.*

"My husband and I had a cottage that we bought about the third year of our marriage. When we got divorced at the end of the tenth year it was just before the summer. I was determined to face it out with the kids in the summer community. And I thought it would be wrong to disrupt what they wanted to do that summer. And I suppose I wanted the comfort of the known. So off we went on Memorial Day for the weekends and then when the kids finished school, we moved out for July and August. I was celibate all summer but I will admit that I was finding a rush of enthusiasm as I relooked at all the men: married, divorced, and single. In fact, I had some trouble with my friends: the husbands were reacting to me as the 'divorcee in town.' But I wasn't having any. Even if I wanted it, it would have been foolish in that small community. And I knew that I might have my sexual needs but I had the need for belonging even more and sex with a husband around there would have meant total ostracism. I met some new people and when everyone realized I wasn't the swinging divorcee they responded by inviting me and the kids to dinner, brunch, etc., whatever; and they became very anxious for me to meet every bachelor around. So I not only never felt alone, I met a lot of nice people that summer. When we got back into the city, life there was a lot easier than it would have been if I hadn't gone to the cottage for the summer. I figure that I made the transition of being alone in the best possible atmosphere, where informality was the key: being the EXTRA just wasn't part of the summer scene the way it would be in the winter. Entertaining was on for the fall and I was invited everywhere. I had a circle of friends that kept expanding and from there I met a lot of men who I started to date. And two or three had been out at the cottage, so the kids had seen them around and there wasn't any problem when Jack started to stay overnight. The kids were used to seeing him and it didn't matter to them if he was there day or morning. It just didn't faze them because they were used to seeing all kinds of adults coming in for coffee, for a drink, for a chat, to take them for a sail, all summer long. So strangers in the house didn't bother them in the city. I was so glad I opted to go to the cottage that year."

Divorced women with children must watch out for the following men:

1. He is divorced, has children, and now his wife is remarried and living across the continent . . . with the kids. Your kids are merely a substitute for his . . . and you don't count.

2. He is divorced, has children, and can't stand being around you when your children are around. It makes him sad and he misses his kids.

3. He is divorced or has never been married; he is terrified of kids . . . including yours.

4. He has never been married and has a false notion of what children are all about and is continually making you choose between him and the kids.

5. He is divorced, has children, and although he is kind toward your children, he really resents them. He gave up living with his own children, why should he live with yours?

6. He gives you attention only because you are a mother. You are a built-in, once-a-week family.

Any one of those types ring a bell? Better take a good look and see what the score is with your latest admirer.

Leila just naturally fell into a situation which was convenient for everyone—until she realized the scales weren't balanced.

"Since he had two kids and I had two also, we spent a lot of time together doing family-type activities. At first that was it; then I realized I was spending more and more time making sure I looked my best for these outings. They were becoming important to me. And then when I got the tingle as he bent over to wipe my daughter's chin with his handkerchief. I wished it was my face. And then I realized it was up to me to get that across to him. It was no problem getting him into bed. Then we really got into a routine. He was seeing other women. I knew all about it. I dated, too. So there were no illusions. But somehow I felt empty when we had sex. Finally I got the point. He wasn't really interested in me. He was just giving me payment for being a surrogate mother for his kids. He was interested in preserving the family group. At first I thought I was going crazy but when he went on a week's vacation with 'a friend,' and asked me to stay with his kids, I finally wised up. It wasn't pleasant to face it but it's never too late."

It never hurts to get the male point of view. I interviewed a number of men and found out about their views about women with children. Reactions to the question "What's it like to date a woman with children?" were varied:

Bob: Tall and handsome, thirty-nine, and restless, he moved from one woman to another as he moved from one job to another. He was divorced, with two kids whom he hadn't seen in ten years. They were three and two when he'd left. He was candid: "I never take out a woman who has been divorced and has children." He claimed it was "nothing but aggravation." I am more inclined to think he missed his kids so much he couldn't face anyone else's. But he was in the minority.

Hal: "Since I have two kids living with me, I prefer a woman with children. We can have family times as well as our own time. And I'm always looking for a wife. And I figure the odds are better when the woman has kids of her own."

Al: "I was married, divorced, had three kids, and now I never see them. So if I meet a woman with kids it really doesn't matter. In fact, I look at it as a kind of bonus.

Fred: A forty-seven-year-old successful lawyer who rode his bike to work agreed to answer some questions if I went bike riding with him. Anything for research, so I agreed. I was sore the next day but I did get his point of view. Divorced six years and not remarried, his kids were ten and seven, both girls, when he and his wife had divorced. "I know kids; after all, I had two of my own, whom I lived with. I never see them because their mother lives in California and I live here in New York. I do miss those kids. So I usually wind up with a woman who has kids. It's not the only reason I take her out, but her stock goes up with me if she is a mother." Since he had been so positive about my question, I pursued: "How do you manage to sleep with her and feel comfortable around the kids?"

"That's always a problem, isn't it? It really depends on the woman and how old her kids are. I usually get involved with a woman who enjoys the family group. It seems to work and then when we become a family, the nights I stay over are natural."

Others answered the same question:

Jeff: "I dove under the bed when the kids came into the bedroom. I was more uptight than she was. She wasn't sleeping with every guy she went out with, but she wasn't making a big deal about it when she was. So the kids really didn't see anything wrong with it. I froze though. She laughed. But I felt terrible."

Craig: "I am living with a woman with children. She was divorced six months when we met. We just started seeing each other all the time and it was natural. I moved in."

Larry: "Women with children aren't worth it. I always have to get up at three A.M., put on my trousers, and go home."

Sonny: "There's no spontaneity with a woman with children. The kids come first. I like action."

Don: "I just can't seem to make it. I have two kids of my own. They live with their mother, my ex-wife. It blows my mind to think that she is sleeping with men. And when I am with a woman who has children, I am always wondering what my wife, my ex-wife, is doing, and that makes me less willing to make it with a divorced woman with children."

Discouraging, isn't it? Well, no one said it was easy. And there is some hope:

George: "If I like her, and she has kids, we'll manage. After all they—her kids—are a part of her."

Don't forget to expand your horizons. Join a group that has been organized especially for you. There are new organizations and groups that are springing up all over the country tailor-made for women with children (as well as men with children). Parents without Partners has been around for years and caters to male and female loneliness by providing social activities where you can meet other people in similar circumstances. Another way to go about it is to look to your church and see what they are up to. Single Church, U.S.A., exists in Orange, California. Started by Reverend Chen after his marriage broke up, he has provided a gathering place for people to socialize, meet one another, and to enjoy. Why not start your own group? Women today are enjoying for the first time organizations that are meant just for them: Momma's in Venice, California, is a forum of information by publishing a newspaper and generally helping one another to coexist, not necessarily with a man.

There are no answers, but there is a way to work it out so you can be both woman and mother. With time and effort and care, with laughter and tears, you should find a way to satisfy all your needs. And once you are in bed with a man, there is no difference between you and your childless divorced sister.

V.

Your Sexuality Is the Sum Total of Your Positive Feelings—About *You*

Sexuality has been defined and analyzed by the experts. I have but one qualification to define sexuality. I am a woman. My sexuality is the sum total of good feelings I have toward myself—that I express to others and is reflected in everything I do.

There is no way to isolate my essence as I get up in the morning, take a shower, get dressed, go to the office, spend a day working, and later associate with friends. The very core of the sexual me extends into all areas of my life—the way I dress, what I say, where I live, how I express myself, my relationships with friends, and of course, how I make it with men.

When my husband and I finally separated my sexuality had been so eroded by the long preceding months of indecision, that I looked at myself and found half a person. So much energy had been spent on the marriage and making decisions and changing my mind (and he changing his) that my sexuality actually receded inside of me—hidden away. My affect was asexual. The mind works in mysterious and strange ways and now that I can see that time more clearly I realize exactly what I did. I was hell-bent on trying to keep the marriage together by not having an affair although sex was getting worse and by being what I thought my husband wanted. That was the worst thing I could have done for myself, him, and my marriage. But it is not unusual. I had turned into an asexual human being in order to concentrate fully on my marriage (or so I thought), which was crumbling in spite of both our attempts to save it.

A broken marriage does work its damage, no matter what the circumstances are. Every time I thought or acted negatively about myself (and there was a lot of self-appraisal), sexual erosion was making inroads. It may have only been a fleeting moment, here and there, but those fragments had a way of gathering a momentum and settling in—to accumulate inside of me as a big hard piece of lead. Not only with sex— everywhere. I had lost confidence in myself as a human being. And I was less than myself in trying to cope. And the toll of all that was in diminishing my sexuality to a big fat zero.

And even if the divorce is the "best thing that could have happened," the sheer torture of the logistics of such a major change (and the events leading up to it) is not without a big price tag: loss of your sexuality potential.

The day he and I decided to split I went into a kind of shock for some time. I couldn't eat. I couldn't concentrate on work or even join in a conversation and keep track of the train of thought. I was in pain. Yet people who saw me at that time said I looked terrific. And in fact when I looked in the mirror, I knew that I faced a new person. I had been liberated. I didn't really understand it then; I should have been dead inside. I wasn't. I was alive, I remember saying to my ex as he delivered me to an appointment that day in the midst of our final "discussion." We were standing on the corner of Park and Eighty-fifth. The wind was blowing and I looked at him and said: "This is probably

90

the worst day of my life. My whole world is changing. But I feel as if a weight has been lifted. I feel exhilarated."

Strange words from someone who felt her whole world was falling apart . . . to a husband who was equally in pain and baffled. (We did care about each other.) But we had finally faced each other and recognized something was indeed wrong with the marriage.

Now I know what I meant that day. In those moments of our final decision, my sexuality began to emerge once again. I was on my own to see that it was nurtured and developed to its fullest.

So it's time to see who you are. Appraise yourself and your surroundings to make sure they represent that which you feel positive about. There ain't no eliminating some negative, but you sure can take the time to emphasize the positive.

1. It's Time for a Check-up: General and Gyn

I have often been struck by the irony of the laws concerning marriage and divorce. There is hardly a state in the union that won't insist on a doctor's check-up and a blood test before they allow you to get the marriage license. But no one has ever considered requiring a physical exam after the marriage is over. I'm all for it. What better way to start a new lifestyle than with a clean bill of health.

Tensions of a divorce often take their toll physically. Don't feel shy about using the wonders of modern medicine if they can help you get through this period in the best shape possible. My doctor prescribed tranquilizers to get through the day without suffering incredible pains through the midriff. Eventually I didn't need the pills but they sure helped when I did. Another woman I know, faced with the problem of being a working mother without a husband, was running herself ragged being all things to all people. Then she couldn't sleep at night. After five weeks of no sleep, she dragged herself to the doctor. A strict allotment of sleeping pills and a battery of vitamins got her back on the road to feeling her old self. (I'm not recommending sleeping pills for everyone, but they do serve a purpose when dispensed by a knowledgeable doctor.)

Even if you're not suffering any visible physical pain or stress, see your doctor for a complete check-up. It can't hurt. And while you're at it, it's time to talk about birth control.

You have supposedly been having sex with the same man for years, months, or weeks. Whatever birth control method you used should have been based on this premise.

Now that you are divorced, there is a very good possibility that you will be having sex with a variety of men. And it's time for you to re-evaluate your ideas and methods of birth control.

It would be presumptuous of me to advise you about the specifics of birth control. You need a qualified physician for that. Consult him and come up with a method of birth control tailor-made for you. It may be the same one you used when married . . . and then again, it may not.

Liz was thirty-three years old, married five years, no children. She had been brought up on the idea that nice girls don't fuck. Now that she was a divorced woman she modified her belief to: nice girls don't act as if they want to fuck. So she explained to me how she changed from the diaphragm to the IUD after her divorce.

"If I wore a diaphragm, a man will know I was expecting to make love, and I didn't want to get *that* kind of reputation. A girl can't be too careful. On the other hand, I did want to go to bed with a man and make love. And I didn't want to get pregnant. So really, for me, it was between the pill and the coil. Then I talked it over with my doctor and he said that I could do whatever I wanted. So I chose the IUD. I mean I just couldn't stand it if some man went into my purse and discovered the compact of those little white pills. I would have been mortified. And the IUD was in and I could forget about it."

For Liz this solution managed to settle the issue

and she had it worked out in her own mind that she still looked like a nice girl. And of course she will never have to miss out on the greatest lay this side of the Panama Canal.

Cynthia had been using the diaphragm while she was married and found no reason to change:

"Since I live in a small town, have two children and a job there is not much chance for me to get sex. And when I do, it's been so carefully planned that there is no reason why the diaphragm can't do the trick. I have thought about using the pill but will wait until there is either one man in my life or if by some miracle suddenly I am faced with a dozen sexy suitors. My situation isn't the greatest for getting laid, you know."

Grace was actually liberated after her divorce:

"My husband wouldn't let me take the pill. He didn't think it was 'sexy.' I tried to get him to explain his theory but that was usually the time he remembered to take out the garbage.

"No woman likes the idea of being 'unsexy.' So I shut my mouth and continued to mess around with that goddamned diaphragm and foam. There was nothing sexy to me about that routine. I know a lot of women swear by it but I wanted to use the pill and according to my doctor there was no reason why I couldn't. It was with total relief and a sense of liberation that I took myself to the doctor shortly after the divorce—and got a prescription for the pill."

That society sanctions childbearing by married women has led many women into misguided laissez-faire birth control. What should be a positive decision on the woman's part, becomes a hit-or-miss affair, while she is vaguely comforted by the notion: "If I get pregnant, we'll have the baby." While it might have worked while you were married (if you see yourself in that description), it is time you came to terms with your body. Now that you are divorced you can no longer afford the pseudo-luxury of casual birth control.

Fortunately for Susan, her doctor was a patient and understanding man who knew her:

"I knew that using a diaphragm was only sixty-five percent safe for me—that is, safe from getting pregnant. I certainly had enough doctors tell me that. I guess it was something to do with how I am made inside. Anyway, while I was married to Bill, using the diaphragm was okay; if I got pregnant, I just assumed that I would have another baby. I had already had one and there was no reason not to have another. We would have preferred to wait at least three years, but it wouldn't have been such a big deal if I got pregnant sooner. We weren't the type of people to face our problems. So when we finally split it was kind of sudden. That's what is commonly known as decision-making by default. Fortunately I realize now I was due for my yearly check-up about the time the lawyers were still negotiating the settlement. I went probably because it took less effort to go than to break the appointment.

"The news of my divorce came out naturally. And I really didn't expect my doctor to respond the way he did. Come to think of it, I really didn't anticipate any response. Anyway, he pulled out his charts and diagrams and starting to give me a lecture on the facts of life. Then he started talking about birth control. He reminded me about the high chance of me getting pregnant. And recommended that I start using the pill. I never even thought of it. But what he said made sense. I certainly didn't expect to have a celibate life and I sure as hell didn't want a pregnancy. I could no longer afford to be so casual about contraception."

Although Gloria's ignorance in matters of birth control was partly due to lack of exposure, that very void was created because she wasn't motivated to find out about it. She was bright, assertive, and lively. But no one told her she had some options when it came to taking care of herself—even when she had been married.

"When it came to birth control I used foam. I

94

figured that if I got pregnant, I was married, wasn't I? We'd have the kid. It just didn't occur to me there'd be any other way. Fortunately for me I was married only six months because I was really pushing the odds —I was due to get pregnant any minute if I kept that up. My husband—it's hard to think of him that way since we were only married for such a short time— couldn't stop seeing his old girl friends and that ripped it for me. I mean, you take care of business at home when I'm the lady at home. I flew to Mexico for one of those quickie divorces. Coming back on the plane I was sitting next to this classy gal whom I had seen earlier in the day—also just divorced. It was a long flight and we talked. About everything. Real girl talk. And then she said out of the blue: 'Do you know anything about the coil?' Christ, I didn't even know what it was. By the time she got through I figured I might as well get a complete education. I asked her about other kinds of contraception. I got the whole bit. This kid knew her stuff. I went to the clinic the next week and got me a whole batch of pills."

It will do absolutely no good to see the gynecologist and pretend things are unchanged. One woman felt she had to continue the pretence of being married and suffered dearly:

"My sister was married when she graduated college and everything seemed to be going great in her marriage. She and her husband had their squabbles, but so do we all. By the third year they decided to have a child. Pearl had been on the pill and obviously she stopped taking it. She tried to get pregnant and couldn't. That lasted about six months and then she went to the doctor. She had tests. Her husband had tests. The whole bit. They were finally told that nothing was wrong that could be detected and they should keep trying.

"Things were obviously strained between them but I really thought they'd make it. Well, I was wrong. Everything seemed to fall apart and it was off to the divorce court. She seemed to be taking it as well as could be expected. It was difficult but she continued

95

with her job and even started dating. When she called me and told me she thought she was pregnant I asked no questions—she'd tell me about it when she was ready—but I offered to go to the doctor with her. I was surprised that she agreed because she was unusually independent. But, when I drove over and picked her up she was near hysteria. I mean, getting pregnant was a pretty lousy thing to happen but it wasn't the end of the world. Finally I managed to get her to tell me what was really bothering her.

"She was afraid to face the doctor. I really was getting impatient with her. The doctor—who was also mine—was really a very nice woman. She wasn't the kind to be shocked or pass any kind of judgment on what her patients did.

"Then when we got to the office, it all came out when the receptionist greeted us.

" 'What are you doing back so soon, Mrs. Long?' So soon? I thought. Then my sister looked like she was going to pass out on the spot. She finally owned up: she had been to the gyn for a Pap smear just the month before and never opened her mouth about the divorce. In fact, she had gone out of her way, for some misguided reason, to reassure the doctor that she was still trying to have a baby. She really wasn't making any sense but from what I could gather, she was humiliated to tell her doctor that she was divorced. It was like saying, I am no longer married because I am not a woman, because I can't have babies, and it's all your fault because you're the doctor and you couldn't do anything. That was a long sentence but it was that kind of crazy, convoluted thinking.

"Well, my sister was pregnant and did go for an abortion. It happens—all of a sudden you conceive after giving up. That deception cost her such pain. Can you imagine what it must be like to destroy something that you had been trying to create for over a year? Afterwards she was so depressed that I was worried enough to get her to see a therapist. She's going now and is on the birth control pills again, I might add. Now it will take a long time to get rid of the emotional scars of that abortion—if ever."

It's possible you might have a good reason not to confide in your doctor. But there is an alternative:

"I was living in a small town when my husband and I split up after eight years of marriage. There was only one doctor and we knew him socially. Although I know all about professional ethics I just couldn't bring myself to go to him and discuss birth control now that I was divorced. I had custody of the kids and I didn't want anything to jeopardize that. Maybe I was being paranoid and had watched too many late movies, but I wasn't going to take that chance. I can't remember the movie but I distinctly remember one male chauvinist judge handing children over to the husband after determining that their mother was an unfit mother because she was having—sex. It may have been a movie but it struck fear in my heart. I really wanted to change to the pill—but that was like admitting to the doctor that I was sleeping around. I am hung up on old cliches. I did the public relations for a company who had a factory near where I lived. Although it was a small town, we were close to three major cities. After the divorce I volunteered to travel even more and found myself away on an occasional night. The housekeeper lived in and took care of the kids when I did that. Then I started meeting men and started toying with the idea of taking the pill. I mean, I couldn't ask my ex-husband's tennis partner about the pill, could I? Then I got a brilliant idea. I changed doctors. The next time I was in the city I called the big hospital there and asked them to recommend a gyn. They gave me the names of three. I made an appointment and with total relief felt more at ease discussing sex with a total stranger."

Embarrassment—real or imagined—is no excuse not to be honest with your doctor.

Even if the gyn doesn't pat you on the back and say "go out and get laid" (and I know some who would highly recommend it), he's one person who might surprise you. Ruth told me:

"I was afraid to go to the gyn and tell him about my divorce. I had been on the pill and I was afraid he would take me off it because I wasn't married anymore. But I knew that it was time for a check-up and I knew that I would have to face him with the request for the pill. I had been divorced about three months and having, if not a great time, an interesting time with all kinds of different men. I was learning about doing things in bed I never dreamed real people did. And I didn't want the gyn to stop all this. You can imagine my surprise when he said to me: 'My responsibility to you is to tune you up; what channel you decide to watch is your concern.' I don't know if I liked being compared to the tube, but I sure dug the sentiment."

And once you've settled on a birth control method, use it. Often carelessness is indication of serious psychological problems. Ida was more disturbed about her divorce than anyone realized and her acting out resulted in some crazy destructive behavior.

"When Jack left me I thought I was the most unattractive woman in the world. I needed men, the more the better, to make me feel attractive. I had one hell of a lousy view of myself. I was willing to fuck anything with a cock if he could get it up. I schlepped from one bed to another. It's all one blur now. I used foam; sometimes he used a rubber. Married two years and probably made it sixteen times. Shit. I was a real mess. I got the pill after the divorce. I'd wander from place to place, barely making it to work the next morning. My purse got bigger and bigger so I could carry anything I might need with me. It was blurred sex without any comfort. Then I started to forget my pills. I'd take one and then forget for a few days and then take two or three to make up. I'd read somewhere that that was okay. But I really didn't care. I was drinking a lot too so sometimes I'd forget that I'd forgotten, if you see what I mean. I screwed up my whole system. But I kept running. I lost weight, I looked a wreck, but I kept convincing myself I was loved because I was not sleeping alone. And I'll tell you, if you're out to get laid and you have no dignity, you can get it anywhere, any time. When I missed my period, it barely registered. I wasn't worried. Those things didn't happen to me. Then I started throwing up in the morning. And I would feel exhausted before I even finished getting dressed. It crossed my mind that I might be pregnant, but I was losing weight, not gaining, wasn't I? And then I fainted in the office and was rushed to the doctor. Thank God he did a thorough exam. I was two months pregnant. Since abortions were legal at that time only if you had the permission of two psychiatrists who would indicate that you needed the abortion for reasons of health, the gyn arranged for the appointments. And I got my abortion. And I am still in therapy. I still have nightmares about what I was trying to do to myself—whatever it was psychologically, the fact was I was out to destroy myself."

So if you don't give a damn about protection from getting pregnant, you're headed for some big problems. It's time you went to see the gyn and the psychiatrist.

It only takes one mistake. Often women who are in the midst of experiencing separation shock or divorce blues just plain fuck up. Whatever the neurotic need, two women I know could have avoided abortions and that psychological drama if they had only used some common sense.

It's Your Move

1. Accept the notion that contraception is your responsibility. (Let the women's libbers yell that it should be the man's; you can't afford to be a test case.)

2. Make an appointment with your gyn (and if you don't have one go to a Planned Parenthood clinic).

3. Tell your gyn that you are no longer married.

4. Discuss the different methods of birth control and how they could apply to you. Even if you think you

know all about it, you could probably use a refresher course. Since new ideas and methods are constantly being revised, you might even learn something.

5. Be honest. Things have changed since the days I felt I had to pretend I was married in order to get a gyn appointment (a deception that the doctor was quite willing to accept, whether out of concern for my feelings or his own inability to handle the truth, I'll never know). Your doctor is not going to judge you and if he does, change doctors. Remember, his business is sex. And gyns these days seem to be some of the hippest people around when it comes to knowing their trade.

6. And once you and your doctor settle on a method of contraception, follow it. It does no good to leave the diaphragm at home when you go away for the weekend or forget to take your pills because you have so much on your mind.

2. Concentrate on Your Appearance

The first step is to stop and take a good long look at yourself—honestly. And make sure you haven't been slipping when it comes to getting yourself together to face the world—friends, family, the kids, and dates. The next step is to go about making some very definite changes. As the saying goes: Easier said than done. But do you must.

I have some ideas where you can start. You probably can add to them. Follow every point in this section. Apply it to you. Think. Act.

I will gladly share my experience with you. At the time of my divorce, I had to take stock of myself. So do you.

Look in the mirror. What do you see? I saw a woman about five feet eight, short mousy brown hair, a little overweight, with bad posture. Whatever possibilities I might have exploited to make me look my very best were being completely ignored. That was the price I paid for a very very sobering last six months of marriage. I had been so concerned with my insides that my appearance had been completely neglected.

I felt I looked worn out, done in, and used. Is that how other people saw me?

Of course this gloomy appraisal was taking place in the privacy of my bathroom. Feeling sorry for myself, I was being supercritical. But there was some truth to all of it because I knew in my heart that I had seen better days. A little melodramatic, maybe. But it was enough to get me started on a campaign for the beautification of Carole. My friend Amanda had responded to the break-up of her marriage by making sure that she looked "put together" every single day. No one could ever tell by looking at her fresh makeup, combed hair, and matching skirt and suiter that she was grieving over the loss of her marriage. But she owned up to me recently when I met her in the beauty shop:

"The day I signed the papers I kept looking in the mirror, in the reflection of windows on the street. I was astonished that I saw the same person as the day before. I mean one minute married, the next divorced. And you couldn't tell that anything had changed from looking at me. It was like the day I turned sixteen. I kept looking in the mirror to see if I had changed just because that day was supposed to be so important to me. That's when I decided to cut my hair. Remember, I had always worn it long—to my waist. Why shouldn't my insides be reflected on the outside?"

Whether you're like me and you decide that there is definitely something you should be doing that you haven't been, or like Amanda, who decided to make some kind of announcement with a change in her appearance . . . read on for some hints.

Mirror Mirror on the Wall

Look at yourself carefully. Is there anything to change just for the fun of it? New color eye shadow (if you wear it), a new shade of lipstick?

Are you making the most of what you've got?

I have never really worn much makeup but a little eyeliner and some shadow went a long way toward making my eyes more alive. And thanks to blush-on, my skin doesn't have to be sickly yellow during the winter months. But these items were collecting loose tobacco at the bottom of my purse—until I looked at myself. Then I went out and bought a duplicate set of everything so that I'd never have the excuse of not looking my best.

Are you sure you're not emphasizing your recent distress by using a too-pale makeup?

One woman I know purposely stopped wearing makeup after her separation because she wanted the world to know how much she was suffering. Her mourning period evoked the proper sympathy but eventually it became a way of life for her—and friends as well as prospective lovers disappeared.

Only Your Hairdresser Knows . . .

I once mentioned to a therapist that I couldn't cope with a particular situation that day because my hair was dirty. Baffled, but intrigued, he pursued skeptically. I explained that if my hair had been clean (in fact it had been only two days since I had washed it), I would have felt pretty, and if I had felt that way I would have asserted myself. But since my hair was dirty I didn't want anyone to notice me, let alone cause a scene, which would surely call attention to my HAIR. After my explanation he suggested mildly that if that theory became popular, I would set therapy back a dozen years. But I am not alone. Any woman would have known what I meant.

The condition of your hair—and what you think of it—can determine a whole mood. And what's so fantastic about accepting this theory is that your hair is one thing in your life that you should be able to control: wash it when you have to; brush it when you want to; and even go to the hairdresser. And the results are immediate.

This is what I did:

1. I made a rule to wash my hair every two days no matter how clean it looked or how tired I felt.

2. I arranged to have my hair highlighted—something

that I had been doing twice a year but had neglected now since I was thirteen years old.

3. I decided to let my hair grow long—no longer to be a slave to the geometric styling of the current fashionable hairdresser. And eventually I would pull it off my face: a final act of independence since my ex-husband hated it that way.

Not only did I look better but I was doing something for myself, so I felt better.

And the results were gratifying. Arriving at a cocktail party about a month after the separation, one of the guests said to me: "I don't know how you feel but you look fantastic."

Hair is an individual thing. What about yours? Have you been missing the beauty shop appointment because you don't care? Is it time you made a change in your hairstyle that people could admire?

While You're At It, Step On the Scale

No matter the circumstances, the divorce is a time of high stress. And it's no news that our eating habits reflect our miseries. For some it's complete loss of appetite; for others it's shoveling down all the goodies in sight. (And if you are one of those "normal" types who stays the same weight no matter what is happening, just consider yourself damned lucky.)

If you've been eating yourself into the next-size dress while he's been busy with his research assistants, stop the self-abuse. It's diet time. One woman said it better than I could:

"After eight years of marriage, two children, and a divorce settlement that took over a year to finalize, I had eaten my way through Baskin-Robbins. I was over twenty pounds overweight. I think the single most fearful thing that motivated me to go to the doctor for a rigid diet was this: getting undressed in front of a man. I wasn't sure I would even get that far but if and when I did, I sure didn't want him to turn off because of my fat stomach. So every time I started to wonder why I was on the diet I would stand, look full length, sideways, in the mirror and see what he—whoever he would be—would see. Ugh. I stayed on the diet until I lost twenty pounds."

I am not endorsing any one method for you to lose weight. Anyone with this kind of problem has faced it before and should know what kind of diet works best for her. Me? I stopped eating sweets, my insatiable urge for anything chocolate, and that was enough to get me back to the weight where I felt comfortable.

No One Wants to Sleep With a Bag of Bones Either

Grace's habits were just the opposite:

"Although the divorce was my idea, it was a rough time. I tried to eat but I could barely finish a meal. Finally I stopped pretending. I'd feed the kids and then pick a little at the leftovers: that was dinner for me. I lost weight and my clothes were hanging on me. It was my sister who insisted I see a doctor to make sure nothing drastic was wrong. Actually she nagged me but got nowhere until I decided to go myself. And why? Well, how would you like to hear: 'Forget it, lady, I like my women with a little meat on 'em.' That from a delivery man who started to make a pass. And before I yelled he had already rejected me. I was relieved but on the other hand I didn't want to be pushed away because I wasn't attractive. That hurt, even from that monster. I did go to the doctor and he put me on some medication and gave me a specific diet to follow so I would gain weight. (I also was more careful with delivery men.)"

It's time to pamper yourself. Go on a shopping spree.

Your first stop should be the lingerie department. How long has it been since you've been there for yourself (other than buying yet another shower gift)? Too long.

I bought all new underwear, one very sexy nightgown, and two new robes.

This served a multitude of purposes:

1. If and when I undressed in front of a man (and I was ever hopeful) I no longer had to worry that I

was wearing that bra that used to be intimate with his red socks in the washing machine.

2. It gave me a certain self-confidence to know that I was wearing matching bra and panties—with flowers yet. My mother always said to me when I was leaving the house: "Make sure you have on clean underwear, you never know, you might be in an accident, and it would be embarrassing." So much for my mother's priorities. But I, as my mother's daughter, will translate for you: Make sure you have on clean, pretty underwear; you never know who's going to be undressing you.

3. It was something I was doing for *me*.

4. Since my ex-husband always bought me robes for various occasions, I was always being reminded me of the romantic night we spent at the Plaza on my birthday, or the obligatory gift given that Christmas. Whether I was spending the night alone or making morning coffee for a recent lover, I needed no reminders of the past, so the new robes—*my* choices—served me well.

And after a long day of weary confrontations, I would come home, take a long hot bath, put on a new, fresh, sexy nightgown, and feel peaceful. Don't ask me why or how; it just works that way. Try it.

Next go to the perfume counter. It's time to change your scent. Now even if you think I've gone off the deep end about underwear . . . and sure, it might be my thing . . . you have to pay attention here. This applies to every woman reading this book.

Your scent reflects your sexuality whether it's baby oil or Joy. We learn to be pleasing to the eye and to the ear and later to the taste, but often we forget about the sense of smell. But it should never be neglected by you.

What can you do? Develop an identifying smell. If you never found one perfume that reflects you, it's about time you did. Go out and buy new bath oil, powder, perfume, and cologne. This doesn't have to be an extravagance. Spend only what you can afford. It's part of the pamper-you program.

Scent by association has its plusses. Once you are into your new perfume, associations can work to your advantage . . . on him. When he leans over in greeting at the PTA meeting and your scent is familiar, he can hardly not remember last night. And if last night was spent with him, who's to complain?

If you know the plusses when it comes to having a smell all your own, then you're halfway there. But it's time for you to change. Why?

By changing your scent, you can help get rid of some old memories. We do make certain associations by smell, without even realizing it. As long as I could remember I had enjoyed using Chant D'Arome. Shortly after we separated I splurged: I was into Bal a Versailles. It was the smartest thing I did. First, since I had had a scent that everyone associated me with, this was a change. And it provoked many approving comments—just because it was a change. I didn't really realize how important all this was until recently. Having spent an afternoon with a business friend, I was aware of being vaguely uncomfortable. The smell in the room was annoying me. Finally I asked her what she was wearing: Chant D'Arome. No wonder I had had a hard time concentrating on the project we were working on. That was working on my unconscious and reminded me of a very very sad period in my life.

Just remember, a woman who will take the time to douse herself with powder, spray herself with cologne, and dab some perfume is telling the world: I like my body. And that's part of projecting the sexual you.

If it makes you feel like a million dollars, it's worth budgeting for.

I think that any woman reading that line knows what I am talking about. Here are a few who did:

Valerie: "Sammy hated me in red and I went along with him—in the spirit of the divorce I went directly to the most expensive store in town and bought a red sweater. Every time I wore it I felt good because I was doing what I wanted for me."

Sara: "I just feel good when I wear something new so I bought a gorgeous suede pants suit to help me face walking into parties alone."

Dianne: "My mother called and asked if she could do anything for me; take care of the kids, visit with me, and I said: 'Mother, lend me your charge card.' "

Ellen: "My finances were a real disaster when my husband and I split. With the kids and my having just lost my job, there was no money. But I saw a scarf that was just gorgeous. I debated and decided that it would mean no movies that weekend but I would buy it. And that weekend we went to the zoo instead. The kids loved it for a change. And I had something new to wear. It just made me feel better, that's all."

Roberta: "I was always terrific at sewing but I had completely neglected it the last few years. I had a sewing machine collecting dust. Then I got ambitious. I got a pattern, material, and made a couple of long skirts and tops. It was terrific: kept me busy in the evenings and when I finally did emerge I had something new to wear."

Day In and Day Out

No matter what day it is or how you feel, you must remember to dress and put on makeup as if you were going to a job interview, on a date, or to meet your parents. You never know where you will be that day or, more important, whom you'll meet. And the last thing you want is people feeling sorry for you. Or making excuses: "She looks terrible, but what can you expect. She and her husband just split." Don't give them a chance to say that. Get yourself together before you leave the house.

Bonnie didn't even think about her appearance until she was faced with the following "truth."

"Even if you are dragging yourself out at six A.M. to drive the kids to school, please don't go out in curlers. You never know whom you will see and even kids have their taste to consider. I drove the kids to school once a week. We had a driving pool. Since I dragged myself out of bed to do it and didn't think I would see anyone but the kids I really didn't care how I looked. I even remember one morning going out just like the commercials that are the *don'ts* of life:

107

nightie under coat with boots and a scarf around my neck. I was experimenting with a new hairdo and had slept with curlers in my hair; didn't bother taking them out. And I was safe: didn't see any grownups to say, 'Oh, my god, there goes Bonnie looking like a caricature.' I only *thought* I was safe. Then I went to pick the kids up that day and bumped into Tony's father, who was divorced and really a nice man. I really liked him. And I think he was showing regard for me until Tony came up and said: 'Hi, Mrs. Samuel, where are your curlers that you had on this morning?' Tony's father got a weird look on his face and became increasingly polite. I mean he had just met me and he didn't know that wasn't my habit. I can't really blame him. Tony's mother had a special problem of never getting dressed and out of bed: very depressed all the time and there I was in his mind, another who never got dressed."

Alice, who lives in New York City, summed it up this way: "Even when I go to the grocery store I make sure that I look smashing. You never know who might be into vegetables that week—maybe a new man: divorced and lonely."

Noel said that I should remind women that even if they are attending the women's group on consumer awareness: "Make sure you're dressed and together. There might not be a man in a mile radius of the place but you never know; you might be sitting next to the sister of an eligible bachelor."

And leave it to Jennifer to put things straight: "I don't even do the gardening without making sure I look good. That passerby just might be handsome, single, male, rich, and have the reputation for knowing more positions than any book." (We both agreed that that combination didn't exist *anywhere*, but she made her point.)

There's a four-point check when you're going out:
1. Is your hair clean?
2. Is your make-up fresh?
3. Are your clothes right for the occasion?
4. Have you dabbed your scent on your wrists, your

neck, between your breasts, knees, and all those other places "they" recommend?

3. The Relocated You

If you can manage it, move. Obviously if you are living in a house with three kids and you and your husband decide that the house is yours, this doesn't apply to you.

However, if you are living in an apartment, it might just work out that moving into another apartment is a possibility.

And if you are living in an apartment, without kids, really think about making the move to get a change of scenery. And get rid of old associations.

And if you have to move because of your new financial status—from a two-bedroom to a one-bedroom apartment—look at the positive side.

And if you can't manage the move, there are other things you can do. This works in stages:

First, get rid of anything that has to do with the man you were once married to. Above all, get rid of his picture on the table. There is nothing that will turn off your date faster than a glimpse of Mr. Ex sitting on the mantel next to your wedding picture.

When my husband left I was a human whirlwind. My aim: to purge his presence from the apartment. I took all the ashtrays out of every room. He smoked; I didn't. I washed every one of them and put them in a closet. In fact, I designated a closet: HIS. And every time I came across something that was decidedly *his* and not mine, I opened the closet door and shoved it in. Then one day I called him to come and get all his goodies.

Some of the things in the closet were: his attempts at watercolors that had been hanging in the hallway; his guitar that I had given to him for his birthday that he had lost interest in; a burnoose that had been given to him from an admirer (female, no less); books that were especially his and those that I had given him; records that only he could stand the sound of; and a

109

few choice gifts from his mother that I always hated.

Then I went into the bathroom and took out every single male item in the medicine chest: every old prescription that had been his; his old razors and cologne that he had abandoned in favor of some new scent; his old suntan lotion (it was not my brand); and the Kaopectate (his problem, rarely mine). All this, into a box, and into a closet.

From there I hit the kitchen and removed from the cupboards and the refrigerator all the food that was strictly his taste (how I hated the smell of that clam chowder when he cooked up a batch for a midnight snack). All the candy, frozen delicacies, and fattening foods went to the next-door neighbor who was perfectly willing to accept them on my pretense that we were going out of town. (I didn't have the courage to admit I was doing the staying.)

I didn't even know whether he'd be back. It didn't matter. I didn't know which way was up and it just seemed the right thing to do. If I was going to make it alone, then I sure as hell should have *my* things around me. I didn't need reminders of him every time I brushed my teeth or opened the freezer.

The psychological air spray is a great way to spend an evening when your insides are in a turmoil and your energy level is up, up, up, and there is no place to go. Furthermore, it's a therapeutic symbolic gesture. And finally, it shows your friends you do mean business (and your ex when he comes to visit the kids).

Look around the room. Put away everything that is strictly his. You don't need that pipe rack around. If there is a chair in the kitchen that was always his, don't be morbid and keep it empty in case he returns. Move into it yourself. And this is especially important if you have kids who are bewildered enough at daddy not coming home for dinner. Why keep them in suspense by keeping the chair empty?

Eventually, if you can afford it, you can make some bigger changes. Get rid of the big armchair that he always read the paper in; finally, sell the antique table

110

that you and he bought on your honeymoon, if when you look at it today it moves you to tears; redo his study into a workroom for you or a playroom for the kids. There is no need to have reminders of him around to haunt you; and there is no need to build monuments in his honor.

I know one woman who was redoing her apartment in order to exorcise her husband and to keep her occupied. She was so excited about visiting various showrooms, looking at fabrics, she really seemed to get into it. I didn't see her for a while but finally she invited me over for dinner and to see her newly redecorated place. It was all different, I wouldn't recognize it, she told me. So I walked in expecting to be overwhelmed by the new her. Would you believe that she had practically duplicated what she had before. The colors different but it had the same feeling. It takes a lot of thinking to make sure that you don't fall into old habits and that your choices are not based on your married thinking. And then I realized where the problem was when I mentioned this to her. She answered in perfect candor: "Yes, it is like the old place, but just in case we decide to go back together." I threw my hands up in disgust. She had fooled herself that time.

The bedroom is a perfect place to make a statement that reflects you.

Any bedroom that was once shared by husband and wife has to have taken on a married feeling (if it doesn't the marriage really was wrong from the start, wasn't it?). It's that neutral feeling that I am talking about: not too masculine, not too femine. The compromise bedroom. Now is the time to change that and make it all woman. And at the same time you will be creating a place for you only.

Fortunate enough to have lived in an apartment when I was married, and unfortunate because I had to lower my standard of living when I got divorced, I moved. But that gave me a great chance to do my bedroom the way I wanted. To indulge every fantasy about myself. (I ignored the kitchen; I had had enough domesticity. The living room furniture from the marriage made do.) But then I concentrated on the bedroom. It was where I spent the most time by myself. I wanted it to be *me*; I wanted to forget my husband, and I wanted a man to feel comfortable in it too.

I got a deep red carpet (something I had always wanted) and even ordered a red phone from the telephone company. Brown drapes were made for the windows. That was the sensible side. Living in New York, I couldn't give in to my true desire for all white.

I ordered a bedspread: with flowers. Since tiny pale posies just aren't my style, I searched until I found bold flowers: red, brown, and white. Fresh, lively, rich. It cost a fortune but it was worth every cent (I still have it).

The sheets: all brown, flowered yellow, striped red and brown. Blankets: all new. Comforter: scrumptious.

No one would ever associate me with blue (when I was a kid); purple (when I was single and living alone); black and white (when I was married). And the NO FLOWER edict coming from my husband was modified to express me.

A note: there is nothing like fresh flowers in a woman's bedroom to make her feel good. And a man takes notice and hopefully will replace them for you (or wonder who your other suitors are).

Every person needs a retreat all her own—and why not make it her bedroom. Especially if you have kids.

Alison had been married fifteen years when she and her husband decided to split. She and her two kids stayed in the house that they had bought five years before. But it was driving her crazy.

"I really got depressed every morning when I woke up and saw the same things I had seen when I was married. There I was sleeping on the same side of the bed, opening my eyes to the same view, surrounded by the same furniture. How dare it be the same when my whole life was changed? And it always took me by surprise when I woke up. Since my finances were a mess I couldn't redo the whole place. But then I called the kids together. Kevin was fifteen at the time; Susan was thirteen. I told them my problem. Then my bedroom became a family project. We painted the room a new color, got some wallpaper that my son put up himself. My daughter helped me sew some new curtains and I made a new bedspread. It took only one weekend and the room underwent a complete transformation. And even my daughter said to me: "Mother, I'm glad you have a place of your own." Meanwhile, my son seemed very proud of himself for managing to do all the things I would have asked my husband to do."

All in all, Alison got a place of her own and her family got a chance to come together and focus on something other than the divorce.

Another woman with kids lived in an apartment. She was in desperate need of something for herself. So much of her energy was spent trying to keep the kids from dwelling on the divorce. In addition, she was now working. And it was in her bedroom that she found solace, but even then something was wrong.

"After a day coping with three kids and a job, the only place I felt I wasn't being pulled and pushed was at home, in my bedroom. And there was nothing like lounging around on a Sunday morning when my parents took the kids for the weekend. It took me three months before I realized that my bedroom was depressing me at the same time it was comforting to be there. The furniture had been a wedding present from my parents. The bedspread had been purchased when my husband and I went to Spain. There were so many associations right there that I was trying hard to forget. I couldn't afford to change everything but I did manage to rearrange everything and even got rid of one piece of furniture I no longer needed—my husband's dresser. And it was simple enough to get a new bedspread. Somehow it made the difference."

Alicia had been married for four years before the divorce. She lived in New York City and was busy trying to find herself. And then she decided to change her whole image. She practically lived at Bloomingdale's

113

as she went from department to department buying new clothes. But she also decided to change her bedroom. When I asked her about it, she told me the secret of her changeover:

"It's all in the sheets. You should never sleep on anything that reminds you of the time you and your ex made love. I went out and got all new sheets; clean and fresh. Why shouldn't I? When I got married, we had new sheets. So now that I'm divorced I figure I deserve the same thing."

Not all of us can afford to be that extravagant, but Alicia was doing things in her own rambunctious way. Nor are we all that open about why. There is no reason why you can't make changes for yourself based on who you are and what your income is.

Another woman's problem was unique, but the way she handled it should give you some ideas:

"My husband had been an art collector so our bedroom looked like a wing of the Metropolitan Museum of Art. I looked at the same painting every morning for five years. And when he left I continued to look at that same spot. One night I came back to my place with a man I had met the night before. We were really turned on to each other. And then I looked up and saw that goddamned picture I had seen in the same position—only last time it was with my husband. I couldn't even have an orgasm it upset me so much. The poor guy I was with never knew what had happened. But I did. The next day I took all the pictures, paintings, and lithos off the walls. Blank walls for me and no more past associations. It worked, too. I felt freed."

No matter how much you love those kids, keep their things and pictures out of your bedroom. This is the place where you are a woman—selfishly so. And if you want to indulge in fantasies of being the queen of the barge or the lady on the yacht, go ahead. If it makes you feel good, do it. Don't feel guilty. You're not shutting the kids out: you can put their pictures anywhere else in the house. To be able to luxuriate in your total womanness, you don't need that reminder of the day you and your ex took Johnny to the new nursery school; and that picture on your dresser will do just that.

And if a man makes it into your own inner sanctum, why put him uptight with a rogues' gallery of your family. One woman, married over twenty years, was divorced. Her kids were grown and she moved to an apartment. It seemed perfectly natural for her to keep pictures of the kids in her bedroom. However . . .

"I'm on the other side of fifty. But I still enjoy sex. And my kids don't live with me so there is absolutely no special problem there. My problems though are like any other divorced woman's. After so many years of marriage, old habits die hard. I was seeing a man who had been recently widowed and my age. Really a sensual male, and we were both turned on and we knew what to do about it. We went back to my apartment the first time together and had a few drinks and then moved into the bedroom. And there were all my kids and their children, not to mention my husband. Since he was forthright enough to say what was on his mind, he gently asked me about them. Then, after we made love—he kidded me about the pictures. But I realized they were bothering him. And you know, once I realized it was a problem I knew they were bothering me too. So off to the study those pictures went, and everything that went into my bedroom after that reflected me—the new me. I had always been an admirer of Jasper Johns and I went and got a gorgeous litho—for a fortune—but it was worth it. I loved it and it made me feel extra good when I was in the bedroom—alone or with my lover."

Brenda wanted a place of her own as well as a place that reflected herself, when a man was there.

"I wallpapered the wall behind the bed, changed the patterned bedspread for a white lacelike coverlet. The end tables I painted white. The curtains were changed from draperies. My husband couldn't stand sunlight in the morning so we had those heavy things made and when I got up in the morning I couldn't tell

115

if it was really morning, or the dead of night."

I visited her in the midst of the changeover and marveled at the transformation. From a heavy, dreary place to a light and airy room. She had added plants all over now that sunlight was available. And it really looked healthy and it looked like her: alive, growing, and bright. She had a place of her own and she also knew that when a man walked into her bedroom, he'd know it was hers.

The ultimate compliment came from her latest love one morning as they were leisurely waking up. "You know, I usually hate to be in a woman's bedroom because it makes me uncomfortable. I had always thought it was because it was 'feminine.' But I feel absolutely comfortable here. And it's still you." And as he reached for her she knew it wasn't because she was masculine, that's for sure.

What he meant, we figured out, is that the bedroom was Brenda. He wanted to be with Brenda. And therefore he liked being in places that reflected her. Up till now, women's bedrooms that were frilly, womanly, or feminine had merely been what *Good Housekeeping* or referred to as their idea of what feminine should be.

So, it all comes back to you . . . and your sexuality. And your bedroom should reflect that—it'll make you happy and it's bound to work in your favor with the man in your life.

One woman I know, a social worker, told me that whenever she was depressed she changed her bathroom. After the bedroom, that is where you should be able to luxuriate with your own thoughts and no pressing responsibilities. Her reasoning: "It was a small enough room that I could afford to complete what I started. And that advice could apply to you. It only takes a shower curtain, a can of paint, maybe a carpet remnant. If you share the bathroom with the kids, it might not be quite so easy. But you can still get rid of reminders of your ex. I never did like the wallpaper he chose when I was away. And if you live alone, or have your own bathroom, go all out and have fun."

VI.

Friendship and Some Other Rude Awakenings

1. RSVP

There are rights and wrongs, do's and don't's that can help make your decision to accept or decline an invitation. But just for the record, here are some questions I asked and have had asked of me about just that.

If I'm invited to a party, do I have to go? I really don't feel like seeing anyone, let alone be charming.

Go. You never know who might be there. And it might be just the thing to feed your badly bruised ego. It's time to make a social life for yourself and to re-establish yourself in your new status. And if you go and hate it that much, you can always leave. I have.

But what if I feel like I've been going, going, and I'm exhausted? Should I force myself?

No. That's different. Don't be greedy. Stay home

some nights. Talk to friends on the phone. Clean out your closets. Read a good book. Paint your bedroom. Pamper yourself (remember, the bathroom is all yours now). Running around every single night is no answer to loneliness. You have to face yourself sooner or later.

Partying can be hazardous for the divorced woman, especially if she and her husband are still living in the same area and maintain some of the same friendships.

My husband and I have been separated three months and I still get invitations addressed to Mr. and Mrs. What should I do?

Depends on the source. If it's a large general affair where everyone will be, you shouldn't miss it. If you don't feel like going, send the invite to your ex.

However, if it's a more personal invitation by someone who just hasn't caught up with the news of your divorce, you'd better face the music, make a phone call, and let them know about it.

What if they ask me if they should invite him?

Again, consider the source. If you are not about to tell them your intimate life details, the only gracious answer is yes.

Then what if I don't want to go?

It's up to you. You can later decline with a gracious and understandable excuse: "I will be out of town that weekend." "Friends of the family will be in town and I must be with them." It shouldn't be too hard to decline gracefully.

But is that fair? Why should I have to say no?

But you can say yes. And if you feel you don't want to see your ex-husband for whatever reason, it's your decision not to go. It may not be fair, but you can't blame anyone. Not even him.

But what if someone invites me and then tells me she invited my ex-husband? When a close friend did this, I told her she'd have to choose between the two of us. She wouldn't. Was I wrong?

Yes. Don't make your friends get in the middle of your separation or divorce. Don't force them to take sides or you'll wind up in the cold.

You mean I should have gone?

Not necessarily. How do you think you'll feel when you see him? If you can't hack it, don't go. But if you think you can maintain your cool (and he his), go ahead.

But if I do go, won't other people be uncomfortable?

That's their problem. If you both conduct yourselves with dignity, the onus is not on you.

If I don't go, will I insult my friends?

Not if you're honest about why you're a no-show . . . or think of a reason to get out of it graciously.

I was invited to a party and the hostess asked me if it would be okay to invite my ex. How should I answer?

Honestly. But it depends on you and your relationship to the hostess as well as to your ex-husband. If you know her well enough, come right out and tell her how you feel. If it's okay with you, then the obvious answer is yes.

But what if I say no?

Well, she asked, didn't she?

What if I say yes and I really don't mean it?

Again, you made the situation. If she is really a good friend, then you did the wrong thing, didn't you?

I was invited to a dinner party—about six people— and I know that those same people had my husband for dinner last week. Should I go?

Why not? These people are your friends, too, aren't they? And it's time you let them adjust to the new you. If they start getting curious about your life, it's up to you to keep the conversation neutral. And remember, don't badmouth your ex or brag about your exciting new life when there's a lull in the conversation. Chances are they really aren't that interested in your scoring points. And if they are, maybe they aren't really your friends.

If I do go to a party and my ex-husband is there, how should I act?

Natural. Easier said than done though. One woman I know told the story about walking into a publication party and seeing her ex with a "drop-dead gorgeous beauty." She just turned around and left.

If you do stick it out, don't make a scene. Your knees may be shaking while you size him up (at the same time glad you washed your hair), but you can still be courteous.

And if he's with his latest girl friend, don't stare at her. After all, it's not her fault you and he split up.

2. Know Thy Friends

Getting a divorce, separating, or even breaking up with the man you have been living with is a painful experience. But it's a dead reckoning when it comes time to find out who your friends are. It's not at all predictable; often surprising.

120

If you're lucky you've got one good friend:

To share your grief. To hold your hand. Whose shoulder you can cry on. But basically it is a time for you to go out and surround yourself with people who have your best interest at heart. If you have been so isolated that no one is around to listen, don't overlook those people who want to see you for dinner, spend the day with you and your kids picking apples at the orchard a few miles away, or who want to go to the movies with you. After the initial shock of your divorce, it's time to enjoy these people and the activities you can plan together. It is not time to dwell on the details of your split.

Don't be alarmed if you find out some friends you had as a couple are no longer calling you:

I'm sure you've got some friends who no longer feel comfortable with your ex-husband. That's just natural. One office colleague of mine, recently divorced, came into my office, closed the door, and said she wanted to talk to me about something personal. She was very upset because she had not been invited to a friend's wedding. Her husband was to be best man. They had been friends with the couple for a long time. After we finished talking, she admitted that they were friends mainly because her husband and the male half of the couple were constant companions to all the football, basketball, and hockey games. So no invitation was nothing against her; it really turned out that they were his friends after all. All the more reason the divorced woman has to get out there and establish her own social life.

Beware of friends bearing advice:

If you are enjoying a normal sex life, there is always someone who will raise an eyebrow. Before you start making excuses or fall into the trap of self-hatred (too easy for the DW), look twice at who is giving the advice. Is she jealous? Is she afraid her husband may be your next lover? Is he jealous that you haven't slept with him yet? Is he terrified you might be giving his wife ideas?

Talk is cheap and unfortunately there are too many people who can't find better things to do with their time than talk about you. And if you are enjoying an active social life and a regular sex life, it is inevitable that some of that talk is going to be about you. If it's a man who gets divorced, the general reaction to his "sport fucking" is: "It's good for you; you're making up for lost time." The shrink is *Blume in Love* even recommended it to the title character as a solution to his depression after divorce. However, when it comes to the woman, reactions often are more complicated and blatantly judgmental: "She's so upset about her divorce, she doesn't realize what she's doing."

Be prepared for all kinds of conversations, advice, and confidential conversations about your sex life. It may not be in your best interest at all. It may reveal a lot about the anxieties of the person giving you the advice. Needless to say, I didn't escape the well-meaning friend who called me to have lunch—urgently. I canceled my plans for the next day and met her at the local deli. She got to the point. We started talking about men, sex, and me. "George and I"—George was her husband—"decided it was time I talked to you. That is, about your behavior." "My what?" I yelled across to her. I was indignant. My god, I hadn't exactly been fucking the whole world. It had been three months since my divorce. and I had slept with three or four men (four if you counted the guy I asked to leave my apartment when I realized he was impotent). I did know that I had spent more nights at home, in bed, alone, crying, than I had fucking. That I knew.

Always attack when attacked, I had learned at an early age. "What do you mean behavior?" I asked even though I knew. I have to admire her; she pursued: "It's about discretion." "About what?" I seemed to be answering questions with questions. But I was stalling this time. I was thinking. And fast. Had I been flaunting my sexuality? Showing up at work three days in a row wearing the same skirt and sweater? Talking about sex with anyone who would listen? Listing the men I had slept with that month and pinning it on the bulletin board? Taking my birth control pill in the middle of an editorial meeting? Leaving a list of abortionists, just in case, next to the telephone? Dragging myself around just before my period, worried—aloud—that I was pregnant and confessing with embellishment that I didn't know who the father was? And if I did, should I tell him? Setting up a poll whether to have the baby or get an abortion? Sighing with relief when I finally got my period—sighing so loud every woman in the ladies' room could have figured I had something to worry about?

From the ridiculous to the impossible? I went back and forth in my mind watching her struggle with an answer to my question. I pushed: "What are you trying to tell me?"

"It's just that George and I have been worried because you seem to be sleeping with one guy and then another. It seems that you won't settle on one."

Whoa, I thought to myself. What's up? George and she are sure in a hurry to get me into a permanent relationship. What kind of threat was I posing for them anyway? Somehow I just don't think this conversation was in my best interest after all. Whatever she was up to, I don't really know to this day. But I really didn't think I had been that outrageously flaunting my sexual patterns. Since I had answered no to all the questions I had asked myself, I was sure. If not me, then it was her. Perhaps she felt I was a threat to her marriage, because she knew her husband found me very attractive. Perhaps he found me a threat because he felt himself tempted by my availability. Once the two of them got me into some commitment (marriage even), they would both be relieved. I don't know. But it didn't worry me once I figured out what was going

123

on. If they thought I was promiscuous, it was their problem. I knew I wasn't overdoing it.

Judith told me she had the same kind of experience with her cousin, who was her age, male, and married. "I met him for lunch one day and he asked me right out: 'When are you going to settle down and stop sleeping around? You're giving my wife ideas.' At least he had the guts to say what was on his mind." But Judith learned then that do-gooders often hid their own worries about themselves with a concern about her.

One DW told me that her single female friend also cautioned her but for a different reason. This time the friend hadn't had sex in over three months and was purely and simply jealous. Another DW told me that she was lectured by a married friend who had entertained thoughts of an affair with her neighbor's twenty-six-year-old son but had abstained in the spirit of puritanism and self-righteousness. It seemed she was carrying that spirit a little bit too far into her friend's life.

Of course, it doesn't hurt to take a good look at yourself and your behavior if someone does bring the topic of discretion into the conversation. To put it bluntly: "Have you been seduced in front of the window with the shades up lately?" If the answer is yes, slow down. It's time to take stock and change. More than likely, the answer is no, I have been doing okay; it's my adviser who has the problem. But even then one caution: Don't fall into the trap of self-hatred and doubt. As a DW, you are especially vulnerable to the admonitions of the do-gooders. In fact, you might yourself wonder where and when and how all this dating and sleeping with different men at different times is going to end. Even if it's only a different man every month, it's a far cry from when you were married to one man.

Cathy went into a crying jag when a friend of hers pulled her aside with "advice."

"I hated the idea that I had to find someone to sleep

124

with after spending six years with one man—and sex had been good up till the last few months. About three months after the divorce, and about five men, I was really upset. I felt that my life was a search for that one good fuck. When I look back, it wasn't so bad really but at that point in time I felt used and dirty and tired. So when Cynthia came over to talk to me about 'what I was doing to myself' she had a willing and eager audience. By the time she left, I felt like the town whore. I cried for two weeks until I got up the nerve to talk about it to another friend who had been divorced two years. Thank God I did. She really made me feel better about myself and I didn't feel crazy anymore. I was so damned lonely, it was easier for me to hate my behavior than it was to admit I was alone, lonely, and scared of being alone.

Eventually Cathy's social and sex life developed into some regular pattern that suited her needs. It wasn't settling into a relationship with one man, either. But eventually she was confident in her own reactions and believed in her own behavior.

Until you find your norm, try to keep some perspective when a well-meaning friend comes to call and gives advice.

3. The Delicate Balance of Male Friendships

Since you're the one who has changed, it's up to you to restore the balance of your relation to every man in your life. And usually it's just a matter of letting him know you are not interested in chasing him into the bedroom, or not expecting him to make a pass.

I'm Available—He's Uptight

I found that I had yet another problem in establishing the new me with my men friends. Suddenly I became an available woman (I had made it quite clear that I was not available while married). Not in any way pretending to understand male psychology, I found that this elicited some strange responses from old friends. Men whom I had known socially or in business, and had been at ease with (and they with me), were suddenly uptight when I walked into the room. One man confessed that he was uncomfortable because he had never looked at me before as a sex object. His words, not mine. That was his problem. Just because I had been married there was no reason to go that far. I put my mind and his at ease by kidding him into thinking that sex was the farthest thing from my mind. It put him back into familiar footing with me.

Another man whom I casually knew actually made a pass when helping to move my records from one apartment to another. And was genuinely relieved when I said no (he really didn't turn me on). Still another gentleman friend tried to avoid me after he found out about the divorce. The situation with him was a little more complicated.

Stan and I had known each other for years. We had worked for the same company and about a year before my divorce he had changed jobs. But we made it a point to have lunch about once a month and talk about everything: ourselves, the office, books, movies, restaurants. We just enjoyed each other's company. And there was sexual tension in the air. But that made lunch just a little more interesting—for both of us. Before I go any further let me say that he had been married to a marvelous woman for about ten years. They really worked at a good marriage and they really seemed to enjoy each other (they are still at it at this writing). My marriage was crumbling but I seemed to be the last person to realize it so I wasn't on the make. We just enjoyed talking and sharing ourselves with each other. Obviously we started talking about sex. First in general terms, then more specifically. Whatever our game was, I'll let the shrinks decide. Although there was an attraction, there were no false notions on either side. The bargain was to talk about sex, not to act on it. Both felt our marriages balanced the kidding around and fantasizing about "what it would be like to be stuck on a desert island with each other." Yes, it was that corny.

When the final days of my marriage came round,

Stan was away so he got the news after the split had become final. I told him about it over the phone. When I tried to make plans to meet him, he pleaded a heavy schedule. Finally, after a number of invitations, he accepted. When I greeted him at lunch the charming Stan was cold, uptight, and unable to show anything but how nervous he was. I was hurt and upset. He seemed so tentative. Then, from the conversation, I began to realize what was up. I can't remember exactly what he said but little things just began to add up. He was running scared. Push had come to shove. The fantasy was closer to reality: I had upset the balance. That's not what he had bargained for, and for that matter neither had I.

In one of those rare moments of revelation I realized it was up to me to assure him that I did not expect him to suddenly move in as my lover. Even if I had wanted that it would have been impossible (he loved his wife, didn't he?). I knew he wasn't into having affairs. He'd discussed the one fling he had when he was so overwhelmed with the nastiness of lying to his wife, and he decided, with my help, that it wasn't worth it.

I had to think. And since most of my best thinking had always been done in the shower, I chose the next best thing. I excused myself and went into the ladies' room. While feigning interest in my makeup (which consisted of blush-on and some eyeliner) I reasoned that if he thought I wanted to seduce him into my bed and he didn't want it, he would become very uncomfortable. If he wanted to spend a night or two at my place I was not about to agree to it. I needed a friend, not a lover. And I certainly didn't need his guilt. It was up to me to make him know where my head was at.

I returned to the table and with all my courage told him just what had gone through my mind. And I ended my monologue with something flip like: "And there it is, how I turned down the sexiest man in the room. By Carole, the divorcee."

He just beamed. Not altogether the reaction I had

expected. Then he said: "Thank God, now I don't feel that I have to start playing all kinds of games. I love you dearly, Carole, but I don't think we should ever start sleeping together. Things should never change between us."

Well, we continued to have lunch and laughter and gossip. But things did change. We stopped tantalizing each other with dreamy fantasies of our making it in the back of a moon buggy. We did continue to be friends but he confided in me less about his marriage. And I kept silent about my latest escapades in bed—good or bad. In fact, when we met we got it down to a routine: "Do you have a boyfriend?" he would ask. And I'd reassure him by answering: "There is no such thing as one man in my life, there are so many to choose from." Or, "I'm working on it." Then we would move on to less intimate details. No matter. We had plenty to talk about. I had upset the balance, but it was finally restored—on an entirely new level. And we were both comfortable again.

Carlie's experience was a little more dramatic. Her husband was a big sports fan. He had season's tickets to every sporting event in the area; cable TV for those that weren't within a fifty-mile radius; and radios for the games that weren't available on TV. Carlie liked sports but thought he carried it a little too far. She started creating her own activities to fill the time he spent mesmerized by players and their scores. And she even found a male friend who enjoyed her enthusiasms.

"Most of us women living in a big city know homosexuals. Maybe it isn't discussed, but there is some reason that he hasn't been married and never talks about a girl friend. My friend was introduced to me at an art gallery opening. And from there I bumped into him on another occasion. We became friends and started making plans to go to the various art events together. My husband was overjoyed that I had found someone to take the pressure off him. He hated to go but would give in every once in a while just to keep peace at home. Now he could watch his precious games, and no guilt to boot. So I now had the perfect escort to the theater, and even an adviser on my clothes. Shopping became one of our favorite sports. Then I confided in him that I was seeing the lawyers about a divorce. I realize now it was at that point we started to see each other less frequently. And when I called him to tell him I had just returned from Mexico (it was four years ago), his response was bewildering. He was aloof, cold, and for a minute I wasn't sure it was the same man I had laughed with over the silliness of the movie version of *Love Machine*. But that was that. He wanted no part of me. And I was hurt."

If she had looked at the situation more carefully, she could have understood what instigated his sudden withdrawal. While she was married she was the perfect companion. Dinner, movies, theater, parties—and he never had to make a pass. After all, she was married. In fact, that had been one of her appeals to him. She should have realized that that was why he appealed to her; she didn't have to face her own rambling sexual feelings that were being untended by her husband. This way she went out and went home. Very safe for her and face-saving for him.

When she was no longer married, she posed a threat. And he didn't want to face it. In fact, he didn't want to see her anymore. The last time she saw him, he was escorting another married woman around town—no threats, no problems.

Dina's experience was slightly different. Although there were some hairy moments, at least it had a happy ending.

Dina was a fashion coordinator for the largest department store in town. She and Tom were always working late, giggling about the people they worked with, gossiping about books, movies, and friends. Often they went out together in the evening when Dina's husband worked late.

"When I broke up with my husband it was only natural that I told Tom. And his reaction was strange. And a new strain seemed to be between us. I thought it was all me because I was such a mess. But what I didn't realize but I know now is that Tom was really in love with me. And he had always hoped that he would be able to make it with a woman. For years he had been telling himself that I was the woman. And if I were available, all would be well in the world. Have children live happily ever after. It worked for him as long as I was married. Can you imagine what he must have felt when I told him about the divorce. This was what he had been dreaming about—but now he couldn't do anything about it really. What was really confusing at first was my total inability to judge what was going on in other people's heads. At that time I was only interested in my own head. Tom and I naturally went out and talked those few nights that I was alone. On the third night, he kissed me passionately at the door. I responded. Hell, I would have responded to anyone at that point. And I did like Tom. But then he turned and left. Abruptly. He avoided me the next day. But finally I found him and asked him if we could have dinner again that night. I was feeling very lonely. He agreed. He was a friend above it all. And then the same thing happened. On and off. I finally got a clue that not all was well. About a week later I was having lunch with a client and over expresso and chocolate mousse I couldn't help but confide about my new problem. (I'd talk to anyone who'd listen and I didn't care what they found out.) But she was a hip lady and turned to me and said: 'You've had enough problems without playing Florence Nightingale to some fag.' It was awfully brutal and I don't think she had to be so cruel but she did get me thinking. I had completely missed the problem. I realized it was up to me to do something. The next evening I refused Tom when he kissed me goodnight. I just didn't respond. He withdrew altogether and avoided me for weeks. Then finally he came and asked me to lunch. At lunch we had it out and talked about our relationship and who we were to each other: very good close friends."

130

Better Friends Than Sorry

And while you're establishing this balance, let me remind you that there are some men who should, under all circumstances, remain as friends. Better friends than sorry.

So to all you next-door neighbors and men in the office, let me apologize for penalizing you for being who you are, but a DW can't afford to get mixed up with either one of you.

Sleeping with someone so close to home can lead to unnecessary complications and limits on your freedom.

Next-Door Neighbor

Marjorie's experience was unique but the outcome shouldn't have been a surprise.

"I tried it with the kid who took a sublet in my building. It was for a month and it certainly served my purpose. My kids, who were twelve and ten, would go to bed, and then I would go across the hall and see my 'younger man.' I was thirty-five, he was twenty-six. But he was so supercool and then there were the drugs. He was continually reaching for a joint. I don't mind an occasional smoke but he was too heavy into it. Once I went over and friends were there. For the cool youth of today, they weren't so cool that night. In fact they were quite cruel. They knew I had been making it with their friend—obviously gallantry wasn't cool. They started asking questions about my age. I felt they were saying, 'You're over the hill.' They made me feel very very old and tired. I never went back to his place and I tried to avoid seeing him in the building. When I did see him I was very uncomfortable. Thank Christ, the month was up before it got worse. I don't regret it now even though I was hurt at the time. For me it was a lifesaver. At the time, it's just what I needed."

Right, lady. But read on to see why you shouldn't take up with the neighbors.

I know, you and your next-door neighbor have been nodding acquaintances since you moved into the building. Now he's decided to get to know you. He

131

offers you the latest best seller to read. And that's all he will ever get a chance to offer, if you are smart. He may be a perfectly normal speciman of desirable male but you must remember to keep your flirtations at schoolgirl limits. Here's your chance to have a male confidant who knows you as you really are—even on Sunday morning before you have time to wash your hair and put on makeup.

I have a darling next-door neighbor. We became friendly when the building employees went on strike and he was delivering the mail to our doors. Now we're old friends. He waters my plants when I'm on holiday. I walk his dog when he goes away for the weekend. We also like to have late Sunday breakfast together—if we both spend the night at home—and discuss the week's events. We take turns: sometimes he supplies the lox and bagels; other times I whip up fantastic French toast.

And when it gets too depressing cooking for one, I share my quantities of lasagna, chicken soup, and chocolate cookies. Some of the loneliness of living alone is eliminated by our co-existence.

When I'm in between lovers, he's a perfect escort to the theater; and when he's sick, I feel needed.

Here's a male point of view: built in. And the no-sex rule is certainly important when it comes to my confessions of the activities of the week. If he and I were making the scene, there'd be a lot less to talk about. I'm not that liberated yet.

And if we did become lovers, the time would no doubt come to part and I shudder to think of the complications living next door would bring. That would be the end of privacy. Why torture myself by hearing him come in at night with my replacement—if he breaks it off? And why worry about him seeing me and hurting him—if I break it up? The permutations of problems bring on an anxiety attack just thinking about them.

Office Male

Anyone who claims to be male and works with you

132

should be considered an allergic substance which could prove fatal to you. This applies to the unmarried or married colleague or boss. Now that you are an available (and vulnerable) woman, men in your office are going to look at you differently. Most men will move from solicitousness to suggestiveness. A few will go through the motions of seduction without any action (or intentions of any); others will try seriously to get you into bed. Any of these men might make good lovers, but not for you.

Office romances can jeopardize jobs and keeping your job should be top priority in your life. Christ, it's the only structure you have these days. And it's a place where you can breathe and function as you. Not to mention the paycheck that pays those bills. You need all that now, more than at any other time in your life. And if it's loving you want, go elsewhere. You know there must be other places to find men by now.

When Nona's marriage broke up the only thing she felt was really hers was her job. She had been working for the last few years of her marriage and she knew how important it was to her. Not only was the money necessary to live on (with kids, too) but she felt like a whole person at the office. But she managed to mess that up too.

"Right after the divorce, I was involved in a project at work that could mean a big promotion. That was really a relief. I was having trouble making ends meet as it was. And a move up would have meant more money. Staying late (while the housekeeper gave the kids dinner) meant spending a lot of time with one of my assistants. He had worked for me for about two years. We were close in the office but had managed to keep our social lives separate. Now we were thrown together and I was definitely hungry for companionship.

"It went on for a few weeks, work, dinner, conversation, and good-bye. And then all of a sudden he made his move. I suppose you could say that I was naive when I tell you that I was really surprised. But it flashed through my mind that I hadn't been loved,

133

held, caressed, let alone had sex, for months. After having the responsibilities of the world on me, the idea of curling up like a little girl in his arms was very appealing. So appealing that I agreed to go to his place and we made love. Good or bad, I really can't remember. I was so busy trying to enjoy it, I don't think I really did. But a routine was settled. I worked late three nights a week and we would go back to his apartment once or twice a week for a couple of hours. Somehow the word got around the office—it always does, doesn't it?—and it made my life miserable. All my friends and coworkers, who had been so supportive, suddenly became very hostile. There was no warmth where I went. And I felt damned isolated. I couldn't afford not to have some support, and just having lunch with some of the people in the office had always been a pleasure. Now it was sheer torture and finally I started to make excuses to have lunch in my office— alone. I had needed those friends as much as I had needed the sex. And I wished I hadn't gotten involved at all. But I had made the proverbial bed and I was certainly lying in it. Needless to say, I took it all out on the guy and sex with him was no longer a treat but a routine bore. Breaking it off is another story. It wasn't easy. And I never gained back my friendship with those people."

Nancy couldn't spot Jerry for the exploiter he turned out to be. She believed everything he told her and it was easy for him to bed her. Not only did she feel dirty afterward but she lost her job.

"I was married for three years and I had a job for two of those years. When I got divorced everyone in the office seemed to be fairly supportive—like a family. One guy in particular, however, decided he'd had enough of the brotherly role. He was married but that didn't stop him from pursuing me right into the bedroom. And we slept together. I didn't see him for a few days because he was out of town but when he returned he made his pitch again. I had other plans. Then, the next thing I knew, another man in the office who had kept his distance was really being insultingly suggestive. By the time a third guy came in to suggest dinner—and he'd never looked at me twice before— I realized what was up. But what could I do? That the first man was your common-variety class-A shit was clear. That he was going around telling everyone I was an easy lay, or would put out, or whatever he called it in that wormy mind of his, I'll never know. But the final straw came when my boss tried it. When I said no, he wasn't as polite as the other. He got vicious. I had no choice but to walk out of that office and never return. Even if I did need the money I couldn't stand the way everyone was treating me."

Her office may be extreme but it doesn't mean that a variation couldn't happen to anyone. If you think that you might lose your job if you sleep with him, don't. And don't even if you think it won't jeopardize your job. There are other things to consider.

Dorothea learned the hard way too. She gave in and said yes to avoid the loneliness and then didn't know how to say no when he asked again. Things were uncomfortable in the office for a while afterward.

"I finally said yes to one of the more insistent men in my office and hated myself in the morning. He was, in a word, a bad lay. But it wasn't that easy to tell him. And to get him off my back was just an added burden of the day. He hung around me whenever he got the chance. I kept putting him off but I thought I was going to suffocate. He finally got the hint but I was always uneasy when he was in the room."

And sometimes it works the other way around. What do you do when you start seeing a man in the office and things go along for a while and then he breaks it off? Can you cope with that so easily? Julia couldn't:

"I started seeing a man in the office and that lasted about two months. He was awfully good in bed and I was really crazy about him. I thought he was the answer to the shit I had been married to. Then he lost interest. I realize how it happens. But at the time I couldn't understand what was going on. I even made a few scenes in the office. Every time he came into my office to ask me a business question I really couldn't stand it when he kidded with the other women. No one knew we had been seeing each other. That was his idea. I guess he realized that it was just a stop-gap for him. Actually, in all fairness, he tried to be nice when he broke it off but I just took it as total rejection. And now the office was sheer hell for me to go to. I spent more time trying to accidentally bump into him than I did at my job. That was taking so much energy that I wasn't doing my job well. When another job offer came along, I jumped at the chance."

She was lucky. Jobs aren't that easy to find. But she also learned a lesson the hard way: you can't mix business with pleasure, I think the saying goes. And the saying is right. It could even be said in another way—Liz's way: "Don't jeopardize your job for a fuck."

Your Sexual Vibes

He seems to be calling the shots—but are you sure you understand the game? And according to Julius Fast in his book, *Body Language,* you send out all kinds of clues with your body. The way you walk, sit, stand, move—that's your body language. And now that you are a DW, you could be communicating your availability. And maybe even, "I am a hungry available woman." Or simply: "I am a woman who wants to get laid." Body language is so sneaky that Mr. Fast makes it quite clear that you can be saying one thing with words and quite another with your body. And if you don't realize this, you might be in for a few surprises.

Agnes was always amazed when a man made his pitch for her for a glorious night for the two of them —alone and in bed. If she had looked in the mirror and seen her tight white pants and black—and even tighter—sweater she might not have been so surprised. She always communicated her sexuality by almost flaunting it by the way she dressed. Nothing wrong with that, but she never realized her "clues." Liz called me, crying, one day and asked why her date had lunged for her when she opened the door to greet him. Pursuing the matter further, I discovered that she had been late for her date (and it was the second time she had met him) and opened the door wet from the shower with her robe tied carelessly around her. And if you think that every man you meet is lusting for your body, take a good look. Are you sure things aren't the other way around? Psychologists call it projection: that you are projecting your thoughts onto another person, thinking they are coming from him. Before you get too upset, better take a look and make sure you are reading the situation the way it really is.

Jane explains what I mean:

"I was seeing a therapist at the time of my divorce. While I had been married I had had no trouble relating to the doctor. In fact I seemed to be adjusting to my new life fairly well with his help. But shortly after everything became legal and Vincent and I were officially divorced, I couldn't even look the doctor in the eye, let alone tell him my innermost thoughts. Why? Because I thought he wanted to get into my pants. He seemed to look at me with his cock. I was scared and angry. I really didn't know what to do. I had read about having sex with your shrink in the books . . . but, my God, not me. I felt really used and angry. I had trusted him. Fortunately for me he was a damned smart man. He knew something was up and started working on it. Finally I just screamed at him to keep his dirty thoughts to himself. That was heavy. It came out of nowhere. Well, we went into that one. I discovered it was me that had *him* on the couch and both of us in a horizontal position. But I was so afraid of those feelings that I pushed them way down and turned them inside out. He had no designs on me. What a relief. It was true that the minute I walked into that room as a Ms. instead of a Mrs. I started looking at him—at his cock—as a sexual, available male."

From this experience, Jane started learning to pick

up the clues to her own feelings more accurately. It's like the story of the little old lady who goes in and the doctor shows her the Rorschach tests. Whereupon she hits him over the head with her bag and yells at him for showing her dirty pictures. It's all in her mind, but he gets hit over the head. Well, take heed: don't hit anyone over the head unless you are sure from which direction these sexual thoughts are coming. They may be your own.

VII.

When Divorce Is the Turn-on— Don't Expect More Than "Fucking"

It may sound peculiar to you, but facing the aftermath of divorce for me was like throwing open the door and inviting in every man I had met in the last ten years to a party where I was the only woman. I mean, it didn't seem to matter what I looked like. What I acted like. Who I was. They appeared in my life the minute they heard that my ex had taken his own apartment. The abundance was just unbelievable. And some of the quality was dubious. Guys who would rather face the subway at rush hour than ask me out before I was married suddenly emerged from my present life and from my past. These opportunists were professional halfwits who all wanted the same thing: a fuck, an easy one.

I was approached by men who knew every trick in the book. It was all hands and lots of con. That should have warned me. But it didn't. These guys really have it down to a science—the exact kind—and frankly I was out of practice when it came to spotting the phonies. If you are reading this right after your separation or divorce, you should know exactly what I am talking about.

And in case you don't I'll spell it out. The exploiters all had one thing in common: my attraction for them was that I was a divorcee. That was it. I'd been through so much of this during those first six months after the divorce that in moments of despair I really think that if I had gained a hundred pounds and shaved my head they would still have been hanging around trying to convince me that:

1. Sleeping with them would solve all my problems.
2. They had been waiting for me all their lives.

I know that's an exaggeration but an exploiter didn't see me as I was, but only as an easy mark. And the awful part of it was that this was a pretty damned good assessment. As a divorced woman, I was lonely and a little too eager to believe the attention and flattery that these types are so good at giving. And they knew it. Every one of them. They used my enormous need to feel wanted . . . for their gain. I told you already—I was all for getting laid. But it was a high price to pay if—and I did—get involved with an exploiter. I felt used. And I was. That I managed to have sex was a bonus, that's true. But I could have gotten it elsewhere and saved myself from becoming the all-time punching-bag of the year. The problem was, I actually believed that they wanted *me* and didn't realized until it was too late that it was my divorced status that turned them on. Linda Lovelace would have done nothing for these guys, but a photostat of my divorce papers would certainly have worked up a good sweat.

I finally did wise up. I developed a gut reaction for detecting the out-and-out rotten types. At first it sent signals to my brain: this guy doesn't see *you,* he is just conning you. He knows you're vulnerable and you want to believe him. But then I would negate the signals and repeat the pattern. I would say yes to his proposals —no matter how outrageous. Finally I started listening to the signals. The gut was getting stronger. I was beginning to tell the good guys from the bad—and . . .

but that's getting ahead of my story. (Here's a fact that's no secret: there is no such thing as a perfect gut. I still made some mistakes. But I managed to avoid some big ones.)

So, short of staying home and getting engaged to Johnny Carson for the season, there is no way to avoid the true exploiter: the man who is willing to tell you anything to get you into bed and then cruelly rejects you once he's gotten you there. It happens to all women at one time or another. But you, as a recent divorcee, are more prone to attract this kind of emotional cripple. First, he is an expert. Second, you've been out of circulation. You can't pick up all the clues. Third, you may be a willing participant, ready to ignore all the signs in order to be with a man, for at least one night. (When you finally catch on, and start making some demands, don't be surprised if he moves on to the newest DW he meets.)

What's so uncanny is that men who show themselves as exploiters are often men you have known for years—as a married woman. And they are the quickest to use that intimacy for their own purposes. In *More About All About Eve* the author—Hollywood director Joseph L. Mankiewicz—suggests that the real motive for "that corps of studs . . . who specialize in servicing, sexually, the newly widowed and newly divorced female . . . I imagine it's a sort of vicarious necrophilia; probably the one they're really screwing is the dead, or departed husband."

Not only does he recognize the herd that flocks to the DW, but he is well aware of her vulnerable position and stake in accepting whatever is given to her. I don't necessarily agree with the motivation—it may be as simple as "Here's a chance to fuck and she'll be grateful."

1. Three men stand out as painful examples in my life

My Husband's Best Friend
This opportunist came and went before I had a chance to absorb what was happening. His no-substance

141

line was apparent only after the damage had been done. He called me at the office one day and asked me to dinner. He mentioned my husband in a natural way and murmured something appropriate—"Your divorce was for the best. . . ." Just a hint of what was going to take place at dinner. Yes, I accepted his invitation. At the time all I heard was someone who approved of the divorce (there were still those around who were all for me trying to "work it out").

We met that night at his favorite restaurant, he ordered me a drink and I accepted although I have been known to get very high on one glass of wine, and certainly pass out on two.

We had barely toasted—"to having found each other," I dumbly recall—when conversation took an abrupt turn to my husband—my ex-husband. My date then launched into a rather detailed character assassination, slipping in a few "you know I love the guy but's." Letting him go on like that—and I'll admit to agreeing once in a while—is not something of which I am proud. But at that time it was music to my ears (that I am tone deaf may not be irrelevant). I was so eager to have this attractive man on *my* side.

He even managed to tell me that he always wanted to sleep with me; that I was sexy; that I turned him on; that he never made any advances because his friend was my husband . . . or had been. And now that I was free, life would never be the same for us. If he had proposed undying love and marriage on the spot I wouldn't have been surprised. Well, I was being set up. And I fully cooperated . . . right into the bedroom. Sure, we spent the night together. The following morning, he was cool to me. But I just figured that was the morning blahs. But then he never called me again. And later I heard from a mutual friend that he was bad-mouthing me. I had been had . . . and it hurt.

My friend Sybil had a similar experience. Hers was a little more painful because it lasted longer. Her humiliation was dragged out over at least six weeks. We were sitting at McDonald's treating ourselves to those yummy hamburgers and talking about divorces. I think the lady next to us was fascinated when she heard this story:

"So there I was: an old friend, and a conversation that I now realize was sick but at the time I was digging it. Far out. He knew where I was at. What would be better than this superstar type telling me that I was too good for Charlie. I must have been crazy to listen . . . to believe him. This was Charlie's old roommate at school, they had been friends for three thousand years. I listened and had another drink. I remember laughing a lot. I was loving every minute of it. I know I talked too much. I am sure he learned a lot about Charlie and me. That really pisses me off. Anyway what's done is done. Let me tell you the rest and you'll see what I mean. Back to his apartment. Had some dope and sex. I stayed the night and the next day he drove me home.

"I had such a hangover that I don't remember anything about the morning. I felt empty all day. I was trying to reconstruct the evening. Then the shithead called that afternoon. He was really giving me the rush. I saw him the next night. In fact I saw him a few nights a week for some time before I caught on. The conversation was centered around my ex-husband. I heard about the terrible things Charlie had done to my date—his best friend. I heard how I was too good for Charlie. Even I was ready to change the conversation. But I still hadn't really realized what was going on until I saw my ex-husband and my current escort playing tennis together. And there seemed to be no ill feeling between the two of them. With a little investigating I found out that Sammy and Charlie had lunch regularly. This so-called friend of my husband's was making love to me by night and breaking bread withwith my ex by day. He was getting his kicks from feeding both of us what we wanted to hear. Right? That son of a bitch was using the situation simply to get into my pants. And getting his jollies by reporting to my ex. I really don't know what his thing was but it was too sick for me. I felt so dirty after that one. I never saw him again."

So, when the guy who has been a good, lifelong buddy of your husband's starts to badmouth your ex as he leans over to kiss you, wise up. He's using you. There is always a jerk who gets his charges out of burning both ends against the middle and in addition taking advantage of your loneliness.

And as if I didn't have enough grief, there was:

My Dear Friend's Husband

Maybe if I hadn't been maid of honor at their wedding I wouldn't have been so upset. Or so unsuspecting.

Katie and Morris had been married for ten years. And Katie and I had known each other since college. Obviously when I got married, the four of us spent a lot of time together. It was only natural that our splitting really rocked them both. I spent a lot of time with Katie and sometimes Morris was around. There wasn't much he didn't know about the sordid details of my divorce.

Okay, that's the background. So let me tell you what happened. Ex and I had only been separated three weeks, four days, ten hours, and I was all for trying a night by myself. There I was: at home, feeling sorry for myself but managing to get through a dinner alone, and was going to try to get some work done. The phone rang and the conversation went something like this.

Me: Hello.

Morris: Did I wake you?

Me: Did I sound asleep?

Morris: Well, you sounded like you were in bed.

(Fast mover, that Morris; three sentences into the conversation and he's already got us into bed. However, I am not aware that that's where he is leading. I continue in all innocence.)

Me: Well, I'm tired and lonely and I just took a shower and I'm going to do some work before I finally go to sleep.

(Now that I see that in writing, it was turning into a

144

suggestive conversation and I was helping but at the time I was just glad to talk to someone.)

Morris: You must be lonely [picking up on the obvious] and I was thinking that you need some special cheering up. Maybe just the man's point of view—the way I see it. Maybe I can help you sort out what's been going on and where you should be headed.

(I plunged on without getting the point.)

Me: I'm just overwhelmed. Everything is falling apart.

Morris: Why don't I come by now before going home . . .

Me: Sure.

(Next thing I know Morris is making himself comfortable on my couch, drink in hand. I am curled up in the chair, club soda in hand. Conversation continues right where it left off.)

Morris: So, shoot. What are the problems?

Me: First of all . . .

And I proceeded to launch into one of my favorite subjects of the moment: *me*. Morris listened. He commented. He got another drink. I began to weep. Morris put his arm around me. It was the first time a man had put his arm around me in ages. Ex-H and I hadn't even gotten together at the lawyers' yet. I was feeling alone. Here was warmth and comfort from a good friend. Then:

A hug and a passionate kiss. Coming up for air, I gasped. And pushed Morris away. Morris was very cool, he moved back to the couch and started to talk. The gist included:

Morris: Carole, you've got to give in to your feelings. You should want to need me. I am good for you. I can make you feel like a woman.

(Carole finally got the point. "A man's point of view" from Morris was a chance for a quick lay in the proverbial hay.)

Now Morris was a very sexy man. At least fourteen things went through my mind as I sat there watching him list the reasons we should sleep together (other than that he was hot for my bod):

1. His wife was my best friend.

2. He was a well-known womanizer, I suddenly remembered, and I was yet another notch on his belt (so easily taken off).

3. He had duped me.

4. I had been unwittingly leading him on.

5. If I said no, he might get really ugly about it. Even tell Katie that I had seduced him.

6. If I said yes, I would never be able to face Katie again.

7 through 14. How do I get him out of here?

Then I decided that honesty was the best policy. I told Morris that Katie was my dearest and best friend. That I couldn't have gotten through the last few months without her and certainly not the last few weeks since I had been living alone. Despite the fact that I thought he was attractive, I just couldn't live with myself if he and I slept together—because of how Katie would feel if she ever found out. Actually he took it rather well and chalked the whole thing up to my false (according to him) sense of loyalty to his wife.

Now I am not putting myself up for the holier-than-thou award of the year. But I did decide that my friendship with Katie was far more important than finding out what her husband was really like in bed (according to Katie, damned good).

In fact, after that experience I made it a point not to be alone with the husband of anyone I knew. Not even for lunch. A lot could be said at the luncheon table that I might come to regret. And as my father used to say, "Kissing leads to bad things" (not very eloquent for an educated man); I say to you, lunching with your best friend's husband could lead to bedding. Even the innocent men suffered, I'm afraid, but it was the only answer I had for avoiding any more near disasters. My first encounter with the male point of view may not have been indicative of all men but I didn't want to take any chances.

Just remember when he calls you to offer the "man's point of view" over a romantic dinner, it will be just

146

as helpful when delivered with the three of you *à table*: you, him, his wife.

Goodwill is often disguised opportunism.

A best friend's boyfriend was no exception. Wendy can verify that:

"It was innocent enough. He and I met at Bloomingdale's. In fact, he was looking for a nightgown for her birthday . . . and a sexy one at that. He asked my opinion. I obliged. All of a sudden we were having coffee and talking about sex, in general, then sex with my ex. Whereupon I confessed it hadn't been so terrific lately. His eyes lit up as if I had pushed a button.

"I knew then and there that he was going to invite me to his apartment to get the book he had recommended earlier. And from there . . . I knew the story. The setup stinks, I thought to myself, made my excuses, and left him with his brightly wrapped packages. He was happy with his girl friend . . . who just so happened to be a friend of mine. They were a couple and I intended to leave it that way. I couldn't afford to lose the companionship and friendship of my friend who I had known since the sixth grade. He may have been blessed with the biggest penis in the world (I remembered the outline from his bathing suit last summer), but it just wasn't worth it. He wasn't the only cock in town and friends are part of life's most important blessing."

2. You're never going to get away from divorce as a topic, but sometimes there's a happy ending

Sonny found comfort with her husband's best friend—a bachelor.

"My husband and I had been friends with him for years. He had gone to school with my husband and traveled because of his job all over the world. But when he came to town we saw a lot of him and I always enjoyed his visits. A couple of times he even stayed with us. Shortly after our separation he arrived in town and called me as soon as he heard about the split. I thought it was only natural that he ask me to dinner . . . I mean, we had been friends. I met him and of course we talked about the split. But not for long. He started telling me about Venezuela, where he had spent the last four months setting up some engineering program. We were flirting with each other and he was terribly smooth about the whole thing. When he suggested I go back with him to his hotel room I was honestly surprised. And I told him. But he was convincing. And I spent the night with him. It turned out to be a nice thing. I saw him three or four times before he went back to Venezuela. I was a little worried that he would tell my husband—we weren't legally separated yet—but I gave in to the feelings I had for him which were warm and good. We had some great times fucking all night, making love, and giggling in bed. And I don't regret it. I saw him again when he came back a month later. And things really hadn't changed. For a few minutes I fantasized that he would take me away from it all and I would live happily ever after. I was disappointed when it became obvious to me that that was not on his mind at all. But he never really led me to believe otherwise. He was decent really. The third time he arrived, I was busy keeping my life together with men who were around on a more permanent basis, so I cooled it with him. There were no problems and I'm glad I had what I had with him."

It's a little iffy to start up with your husband's best friend, but if the chemistry's there, it might be worth the gamble. It was to Sonny and no one was the worse for it.

Another woman, Maria, found a great lover in an old friend, a married man whom she had met in business years ago.

"It suited me just fine to see him once a week. Naturally we talked about marriage and divorce. And I gave him detailed reports on my changing feelings. We had dinner, we went back to my apartment, we fucked, and he left. There were no commitments, no anxieties, no problems. That he was married was per-

148

fect for where my head was at, at that time."

You might not be up to making it with married men, but for Maria it was just the thing to keep her from going crazy while she was trying to establish her own sexuality again.

Liz astonished me when she told me that one of her favorite loves of the six-month period was her friend's young brother.

"It was a terrific setup. I had known him since he was a kid. A kid no longer, I can tell you. When I got divorced I was twenty-five. He was eighteen. We had always had a running flirtation with each other. I mean he never put me in the grandmother category exactly and I had ideas about him before I ever realized my marriage was about to collapse. I was visiting her when her brother walked in. And wow. It hit me right over the head: and those tight jeans capped it. At first I hesitated because I didn't want his sister to get uptight. Then I realized that she didn't have to know.

"When he heard about the split he was very sympathetic and went into a whole number about his views on marriage. He was seeing a girl at the time ("his woman") but they had agreed that fidelity to each other was not essential for their love. In fact, we got into a whole discussion about what living with a member of the opposite sex really was like. He had never really done it. I had been married for four years. He was amazed that I really liked depending on my husband for certain things and liked my husband to expect certain things from me. Little things. Although he—Jack, my ex—and I both worked we managed to spend time together doing the household chores. But despite the division of labor, if you will, certain things he did. Like when I ran out of cigarettes at midnight, he'd go to the store for them. And I would make sure that he had something to eat when he had to stay in the city and work late. These were very special moments of intimacy for us. Kenny was interested and listened. And then he started to talk about the responsibilities involved. Then sex, of course, got talked about. Fidelity was not his thing at all. He and his girl had decided it was cool to fuck when you wanted. My husband and I had split because—according to him—he'd found out I had had a short (two-day) affair with a man I had met while he was on a two-month business trip. Kenny thought this was incredible. Anyway the whole idea of discussing sex with him just turned me on. This kid whom I had known for years. And his sister was my best friend. Anyway, he looked at me and that was it. I knew we would wind up in bed. And we did the next day. I called him. And he came over. And we were in bed before we even had a chance to talk or take off our clothes. What he didn't know was certainly made up for by his enthusiasm. And that didn't do me any harm at that time in my life. Eventually it got boring and I broke it off. But he was cool. I think he understood in his own way where my head was at at that time."

And don't ignore the "older man" either. Norma Anne didn't say no to a friend of her parents who called to inquire about her well-being. And it was her divorce that brought them together.

"My parents had been heartbroken by the news of my divorce and were full of the usual questions, don't's and do's. Maybe it was really a relief since they hated my husband. And naturally it became the big news at home. I lived in Chicago and they lived in Detroit. Then shortly after I let them in on what was going on in my life, I got a phone call at the office. It was a business associate of my father's—a senior member of his architectural office. He called, he said, to ask how I was and to invite me to dinner. I went as an obligation partly and partly because I couldn't face another night with some creep who was going to lunge at me from across the room (or at home alone reading a lousy book). That I was about to wind up in bed was the furthest thing from my mind. I had last seen this man when I had gone to my brother's wedding and I had been in my late teens. He had seemed ancient to me then.

150

"At dinner we talked a great deal. He told me about his wife, who had died the year before rather unexpectedly. We talked about my husband—now living in Paris with his girl friend. And we talked about loneliness. There was a great deal to talk about. He really seemed to understand where my head was at. I was twenty-five and he was fifty. Yet there was a special communication. We did wind up in bed and it seemed like we were both discovering sex for the first time. We spent the next three days together and he managed to come in to Chicago "on business' a couple of times a month. It was great for both of us."

I wouldn't argue with that, would you?

3. Lawyer, Doctor or Boss: What if he Makes a Pass?

At the time of the separation and divorce, I found myself dealing with a number of professionals that I had always seen either with my husband, or at least they knew to send the bills to my husband. I was known as Mrs. Sims at work. That this leads to a hands-off policy is not necessarily always true, but in my case, I gave off no hints that I was interested in anything extracurricular while I was married and for the most part my relationships with these men were cordial, faintly flirtatious, and limited.

But suddenly I was an available, unattached woman! And some of them reacted to that. And in all fairness, I had been liberated sexually—in my head—and could only be sending off those kinds of messages: I am a sexual woman. I want to get laid. Something like that. So not only was I sizing up every man as a potential playmate, I had lifted the bans and they were sizing me up as well.

In truth I was totally unprepared for the new currency between us. Whom am I talking about? The doctors, the lawyers, the accountants, my professional colleagues, and any other men who had once known me as Mrs. and were now adjusting to me as Miss (or Ms.).

So, if you do catch one of these "services" turning

151

on to you, spending that extra time, there are three possibilities:

1. He is really seriously interested in you as a woman.

2. He is an exploiter who sees a chance to advise you in more ways than the shingle on his door announces.

3. He is merely being friendly and you are just noticing it because you are available.

If you are not interested in his advances, coy or blatant, then don't let it go any further. Setting the limits now can be fairly simple; it might not be so easy later on.

However, if you are vaguely intrigued, how do you tell which it is: an opportunist's offer, a friendly gesture, or a genuine sign of masculine interest (beyond the platonic)?

There are no rules. It's up to you to decide. Good luck. But watch out for the exploiters. They are often packaged as vaguely normal men who have known you for years on a professional basis but turn into the id-driven Mr. Hyde when faced with the divorced you. And the subtleties of this are endless.

And make sure you are prepared to replace him as your accountant (lawyer or doctor or boss) if you are inviting him into your bed. Frankly, it would be more difficult for me to find a new accountant than it would to find a good lay. If you have drinks with your accountant and you know his reputation with women, you may be balancing his little black book while he should be balancing your taxes. And if you have met your therapist for breakfast twice a week, and wind up in bed, you both are crazier than you thought.

Caroline, a twenty-five-year-old high school teacher, felt that she had to tell her principal that she was getting a divorce. The principal was very kind, and when extra schedules for teachers were handed out, Caroline found that she was given the easier classes. She felt that the principal had done this purposely, knowing that she was going through a "bad" period.

When the divorce decrees went through, Caroline made an appointment with the principal to tell him. She felt that she owed him that much. He was delighted that she would confide in him. Then he suggested that he drive her home that night. Caroline, very hip, recalls the rest:

"I knew in a flash that he wanted payment for that easier class schedule. And I also knew that he was "happily" married with a wife and three children. Furthermore, I simply could not face him or the school the next day if I had had sex with him the night before. But what a delicate situation: if I refused he could make life miserable for me. If I accepted my life would be equally miserable. Touchy. He drove me home that night and I fled from the car with a comment about having friends waiting for me for dinner. The next time he offered me a ride home I refused, but I couldn't help noticing the look in his eyes when I said no. It was a disappointment, and also the 'I'll give you one more chance' look.

"Finally, one day after a week or two of my refusals, I saw no alternative: I made an appointment to see him in his office—on neutral ground. I told him I was purposely avoiding being with him; that I found him pleasant and even sexy; but I had a very strict rule that I would never, never see married men because I couldn't afford to be hurt. You know, it's really funny. He accepted this, and I didn't have any more problems with him. Oh, he still winked at me occasionally and at some teachers' luncheons he has put his hand on my knee. But I just chatter to everyone in general and refuse to acknowledge the old hand action. I put up with him but I knew that he could change at any moment, and I would have to get transferred.

"Believe it or not, I did it with the help of the principal. He was relieved that I was leaving and a little hopeful that if I left his school, I might consider him as a lover. Frankly I didn't discourage this. Maybe you think it's cruel, but look—I had to support my son and myself and I couldn't afford to lose my job. He did call me a few times the next semester, but I was cool. He got the point."

No doubt, the dirty old man in Caroline's life is practicing his knee-hand action on some young thing, but at least Caroline is in a new environment where she is accepted for who she is and not as the new game in town. It worked out well because Caroline had called the shots from the very beginning.

Susie wasn't so lucky with her accountant. He turned out to be an opportunist . . . and it wasn't the ledger he was intent on exploiting.

"Let me start out by saying that if I hadn't had such a miserable day I probably wouldn't have accepted the dinner invitation with my accountant Danny. But the point is I did say yes. And I will also admit to being very very flirtatious with him in the restaurant. I was trying to discuss the incredible problem of financing two kids through school, with the child support I was getting, as well as the pay I was bringing home, thinking that Danny had all the answers. Instead he had a question that blew my mind:

'I wonder what it's like not to be getting it regularly.' That with an affectionate—or not so affectionate— squeeze of my hand. I thought that went out with crew-cuts and bobbysox. The whole thing was too unbearable even to clear up. I mean, one, would he say that to a single girl he was seeing? I'll bet not. Two, what did he expect me to do? Cry all over his carefully creased pants? And three, what made him assume that I was getting it so regularly, as he put it? In fact, the last six months of my marriage were hell: Jim just didn't turn me on, and the feelings were more than mutual. I might as well have been living in a nunnery for all the sex I was getting.

"Anyway, Danny kept after me—pursued. I heard cliche after cliche. I knew what he was leading up to, and I wasn't going to stick around for the finale. I just left him in the restaurant pondering why I would not sleep with him since, one, I was no virgin anyway (yes, he really did say that) and two, I was obviously sexually

154

marooned (to use Dr. Reuben's phrase) for the last six months.

"Anyway, the shmuck forced me to change all my financial stuff to another accountant. No easy feat. In the middle of this mess. But I had to. I didn't want that man to know what I was up to, and more important, I didn't want him making any decisions for me after I had turned him down. Even if he wasn't the malicious type, it just didn't seem like a good idea."

She took the risk, flirted, and lost. They say no wrath like the woman scorned—ever turn down a man? Or let me put it this way: how would you like to turn your dentist down at night and have him drilling by day? Not me. I'm no masochist. If you have drinks with your dentist and he is attracted and unmarried . . . good luck.

Jackie: "I accepted a dinner date with my dentist. After all, he was really nice, he knew me only slightly, and he was very kind. I was obviously so upset when I saw him at my last appointment, and this time I went into his office and burst into tears. When I told him that Sam and I were divorced, he asked me all kinds of kindly questions and it felt so good to talk to him. Then we went to dinner. But then he started calling me at home, suggesting that we meet again. So I did meet him and he confessed that when he asked me for dinner the first time it was only to talk, but he had been thinking and I got the whole routine—things weren't going so well with his wife . . . blah, blah, blah. He was terribly attractive . . . and he did say all kinds of nice things . . . so we went back to my apartment and made love. But all the time he was there I couldn't help thinking that he didn't look—you know—right without his white jacket. Here was a man who had spent hours looking in my mouth, exploring my whole body. Well, I saw him a few times afterward and I am not sorry. He taught me all kinds of new positions and even bought me a wonderful book. Finally we just drifted apart. But you know when it came time for me to have my teeth cleaned later that year I had to find a new dentist. I still haven't found a dentist as good, but I can't face going to this man's office. I guess . . . well . . . I *guess* it was a fair trade."

Jackie made her decision: she got some good lessons for her new sexuality and she had to find a new dentist. It was worth it to her. How about you?

If you have drinks with your lawyer and he is married and you know his wife and it becomes a regular thing, be prepared to find another lawyer. You can't be paying him the kind of fee which demands that much sympathy and scotch.

But then if he was recently divorced himself, you may be in for a treat. Mary Lou was lucky enough to find herself a lawyer who was three months ahead of her in receiving his final decree.

"I've been divorced three years. And I remember I had sex with my lawyer. I can't see where it did me any harm, but I can't say it was the right thing to do, either. We were, to put it bluntly, using each other.

"It was the second experience I had since I was divorced. He was also getting a divorce. We were just two lost souls. I knew it was something special. Obviously he knew the circumstances of my divorce and he went out of his way to make me feel good about myself. And he was grateful for my attention.

"It seemed natural at the time. I can say this with candor: if he were to approach me today I wouldn't want any part of him. Now I can be choosy. And I want something more than just attention. That movie, *Sunday, Bloody Sunday,* said it for me: 'At one time, anything is better than nothing, but then it comes to a point when nothing is better than anything.' Amen."

Mary Lou took the risk, and it was a mutually pleasing affair.

4. Even A Stranger will Get Into the Act

"Divorce" often provokes unusual responses from total strangers. It's a risk to say yes, but finally, it's up to you.

All women seem to suffer the innuendos and the

childish double-entendre remarks from some men, but the newly divorced woman serves to bring out the worst in someone whom you'd least expect it from. And this worn claim to fame is the way he lights up when he learns you've just split.

Judy was jolted by the language that the bank manager used when she went to close her account—the joint account. He muttered something about giving her free of charge "a new joint—on account." When she noticed the hardness rising from his worn blue suit, sitting next to her in the austere bank, she got the gist of his statement. Her uncontrollable giggles seemed to cool his wit and deflate his cock.

Lois found her laundry man making deliveries with a leer, and one day he even suggested that the sheets were clean and why shouldn't the two enjoy them. She changed cleaners.

Sandra got her shock from the elevator man in her building: "What's good for the goose is good for the gander," he muttered as he lunged for her between the sixth and fifth floors. She jammed him in the stomach, kneed him in the balls and arrived in the lobby composed. She never had any trouble after that.

The sick strangers are everywhere. Here you are: Divorced? Right. Vulnerable? For sure. A little more talkative than usual? Well, yes. Just a little overwhelmed by the whole thing? Yep. A woman? Absolutely.

Put it all together and you have a lonely, eager, and defenseless woman. I don't mean you are without guile or the ability to take care of yourself—but I do mean defenseless in that you have not yet had time to build up those defenses that automatically turn off the sick strangers. That will come in time. Meanwhile, you are without defense. To be taken unawares can be very discouraging. When it happens, have a good cry. And remember not all men are like that.

Alice had long blond hair and a tall slim figure. It obviously did appeal to her husband, Jack, who ran off with his—would you believe—secretary. She recalls the day it happened in detail and remembers the first proposition:

"It was a gorgeous spring day. I remember the sun was shining for the first time in weeks. Jack had been out of town all week and he had come home very late the night before. When I got up in the morning he was already dressed. That in itself was cause for alarm. He always slept much later than I did, especially during the week. Then he said he wanted to talk to me. I just knew this was it. Something hadn't been right between us for a long time but I could never get Jack to talk about it. It was just like him to get me in the morning—absolutely my nonthinking time of day. But I can tell you I became alert pretty damned fast that morning. We talked for two hours and then I asked him to leave to give me time to think. I really didn't know what I wanted. He was telling me about this girl that he had been seeing and he really liked her and he really liked me and he didn't know what to do. Well, how the hell should I know what he should do? I just wanted time away from him to digest what he was telling me. So he left. And then as soon as he left the room, the living room became stifling. I had to get away from the place that Jack and I had lived for the last four years. I put on my coat; I remember thinking that this was the first time in ages I hadn't needed a raincoat and boots. Since we had been living in the city we didn't have a car. So I walked out to the main avenue to hail a cab. I was going to go to the office of my dearest and closest friend. I really needed a shoulder to cry on. So I hailed a cab. The driver got really nasty when I told him where I wanted to go. It wasn't in his direction or something. I couldn't believe it. He was giving me this line and my whole life was falling apart. So I just blurted out and I know I was on the verge of hysteria: 'For Christ sake, take me where I want to go. My husband just left, don't give me any more grief.' It was the first time the cab driver had ever heard that one. He was so surprised he just started to move the cab in the direction I wanted to go. So I snuggled into the back seat, biting my tongue to keep from crying. Then, and believe me, it really happened, I heard from the front seat: 'Listen, lady, you want to come back to my place? I'll give you some comforting.' I didn't answer. Maybe I hadn't heard it right. 'Don't get uppity with me. What you need is a little loving.' Well, by then I knew that I had heard right. Can you believe the nerve? Well, I just let out a wail and he couldn't get a word in edgewise. But the nerve. Here I am ready to do myself in and he's propositioning me. When we got to my friend's office, I paid him and jumped out without a word. I was so rattled I even tipped him."

Some of these proposals—or should I say propositions?—may prove to be interesting. And you may want to see what it's all about. But be careful. If you enjoy getting your sex with the guy who is delivering the furniture that day, it's up to you, but don't expect to be anything more than a stop on his route that day.

If letting the electrician cop a feel means that you're now on the light brigade's black book—and they are calling you at all hours—it's your own fault.

These mini excursions into sex could turn out to be a lot more trouble than they're worth. Rhoda had had a long day; She'd moved from one city to another. She was feeling very, very alone when the man came to deliver her bed. He set it up for her and then suddenly she was in it—with him. In her own words she finishes this story: "So we had a three-minute sex scene. He really got it off pretty fast. I wasn't even wet between the legs. I couldn't believe it all happened so fast. In fact, I was so tired I took a shower and went to bed without finding the sheets and making up the bed. But if I had any illusions that I hadn't had my pants taken off by the bedman, it was all very real the next day when he appeared at the door—evidently at the end of his delivery day. There was no question—he wasn't going to get past the door. I wasn't prepared, however, for the way he was not prepared to go away. He stood there shouting obscenities at me and then I remember: 'Lady, you ain't no virgin. I know cause I was in ya. And I'll tell you, I'm the best thing you could get since you was married. You was used.' He kept saying over and over that I was used. He didn't do much for my reputation in the neighborhood. I finally got him to go away by not answering him. He made appearances every day for about a week. I couldn't call the police because I was so embarrassed. I had had sex with him once. And that seemed to give him license to call me a whore. Finally he just got tired and never came back. But every time I see my next-door neighbor I wonder if she isn't looking at me a little strangely—I mean, if she heard that conversation she would certainly think I'm crazy."

The sick strangers will find you wherever you are. Your vulnerability draws them like vultures. Most of these men are trying to put you in a degrading position. They are attacking you when you are down. If you want to indulge yourself by feeling insulted, go right ahead. But it would be more constructive if you realized that it is their head—their sickness—to want to get you when they think you're down. Then, if you do get involved, and it turns messy, like Rhoda's experience, chalk it up to experience. But don't for a minute believe that experiences with all men are going to turn out that way. There are other men around—those whom you can get to know before you say yes.

Reminder—this is a temporary status. The first few months of being divorced. All men are not like this. And for that I am eternally grateful.

5. Beware of Blind Dates

Having acquired that status of recently separated or divorced, you can hardly avoid that age-old custom of getting "fixed up." If you thought you were finished with that when you left school, you're wrong. Friends, acquaintances, and a body of do-gooders will at once be on the lookout for a replacement for your ex (would it were that easy) or at least a date for a pleasant evening. Often this is as, or more, disastrous than it was those many years ago at school. Unfortunately, these matchmakers are more anxious to see you busy for the evening than they are willing to see if the man is decent, let alone on your wave length.

But for now, go. You have to. You may be in for a lousy evening; you may have a wonderful time. You may wind up in bed out of lust or indifference. It really doesn't matter. For these six months in your life you have to be willing to participate in the merry-go-round of variety.

When you go and it turns out to be every woman's nightmare of a blind date, don't take it personally. Do reconsider your friendship with the people who gave him your number. But give them the benefit of the doubt. Maybe they really didn't know him and they were really thinking of you.

Getting fixed up or accepting a blind date can be full of surprises for a DW. Unfortunately, unlike her single sisters who have been putting up with some ploys from men for years, she has to catch up and catch on. Sometimes it's possible to see trouble ahead just by the phone conversation. Furthermore, there seem to be lots of men around who are willing to get fixed up because they are those dirty old men, the exploiters, who can't wait to dial your number when they find out you're divorced. And some of them even show their hand up front—if you're quick enough to pick up on it.

Since few men are brave enough to greet you with "Let's fuck" (Portnoy notwithstanding), and most men think they have to "trick" you into the bedroom (that an exploiter is also a trickster is generally true; in both cases immature exploiters view women as second-class citizens).

One night I dragged myself home from work after a truly exhausting day, swearing all I wanted to do was take a shower, wash my hair, and go to bed. Then the phone rang. It was a friend of a friend. He asked if I was busy and if I would like to see him. Suddenly the aches and pains were gone and my mind flashed on the new pants suit in my closet. I breathed a sigh of relief that he'd called after I had washed my hair. In other words, I'd love to. Then he said: "Well, I'll come over to your place and we'll see what to do." The important words, I realized later, were "we'll see." It really meant: Let me into your place, and I'll make my move. I wasn't quick enough to suggest meeting him somewhere, or insisting on the plans first (although I don't know if that would have made a goddamned bit of difference). Anyway, he came over. We made some conversation. I gave him one, then two, then three drinks. And I realized we weren't going anywhere. He made his move all right. And again, I should have expected it. But I was too overwhelmed by his awfulness to do anything but sit there and watch him drink (I wasn't having anything but soda). I kissed him a few times and finally realized he just didn't turn me on at all. When I asked him to leave, he was brutal: "You whore; you led me on. And you said you were lonely." Well, we had talked about divorce. He had been divorced about two years before. But I didn't realize that my admitting loneliness meant I would sleep with him. He thought it did. Since he turned me on as much as paregoric, I wasn't about to say yes. He left and I felt miserable afterward. I finally got to bed—alone.

Less confusing and more obvious is the man whose conversation goes like this:

"Hi, is Susan there?"

"This is Susan."

"Well, I got your name from George, who's a friend of mine. My name is Sam."

"Hi, Sam, how are you?"

"I feel great. I thought I would come over and visit for a while if you're not busy." (Or, "Are you in the mood for company tonight?")

Your clue: "Come over and visit. . . ." He has never met you and he wants to visit you. What do you figure he wants out of the evening? If you have him come to your place, and there is a big couch in the living room, you have nothing to do when he gets there but sit on it and, no doubt, be attacked. You may not be, but why chance it? After all, he may be as sexy as the eighty-eight-year-old man next door, and who needs to have him playing with your buttons?

And even if he's a guy you met once and you vaguely remember him as having two arms, two legs, a head, and a crotch, consider if you want to get laid that badly. His style is pretty selfish. Can you take it?

You say: "Well, I would love to see you, why don't we meet for lunch next week."

"But I really want to see you tonight."

"Well, where can I meet you?"

"At your place."

"No, I have to go out anyway, so why don't I meet you at Allen's."

Now, if the guy is strictly look for sex with a face and body he doesn't know, and presses to come to your place, just get rid of him. This eagerness you don't need. Something must be wrong with him. But if he agrees to meet you at Allen's, okay. It might be a night to remember yet.

VIII.

And Some Other Things

1. Where?

At that point in the evening when you know you and he will shortly be in bed together, the question, then, is: where?

If you have children and there's a babysitter to consider, then obviously your place. And once you are there, make sure you have things under control so that neither your lover nor you will be too uptight to enjoy yourselves. Hannah's kids, aged nine and ten, have rules to follow: "They are the same ones that they had when I was married. The kids are forbidden to come into my bedroom when the door is closed without knocking. And I do have a latch on it, just in case!"

Another woman with kids told me she always goes to *his* place because she is too nervous with the children in the next room. "Although I sacrifice the feeling of being able to spend the entire night next to my lover, by going to his place for a few hours and then going home, I find it's the only way I can reconcile all my conflicting feelings of what's right to do."

The answer is, then, *do what's right for you.*

If there are no kids involved, the decision is easier:

● if you are in the mood to pretend you're out of town, his place

● if you feel the need for the security of your own bedroom for the right mood, your place

● if the cleaning lady is coming in the morning and she also cleans your ex-husband's business associate's apartment, his place

● if you have forgotten your birth control pills or diaphragm, there is no question—your place

2. How Long?

If you have been married for the last six months, seven or fifteen years, hopefully you have had the security of sleeping through the night with your husband. Now divorced, consider the following:

After dinner and a party, it was only natural that you went back to your house. It's three in the morning. You are both spent after a few hours of lovemaking, then he says: "Where are my shoes? I have to leave now."

For whatever reason, there are some men who will never spend the entire night in your bed. This man will get up in the middle of the night (or early in the morning), get dressed, and make the journey home—leaving you alone. This abrupt leave-taking is often disturbing, specially if you aren't used to it or expecting it. If there is good reason, you have to understand. One man I know had to be home at eight-thirty to receive his children for their weekly Sunday visit. On the other hand, some men just won't make the commitment for even a night. Still others, having scored, turn into rude, selfish children. Whatever the reason, it is always a surprise.

Hopefully it won't happen, but if it does, be assured, you're not alone. Your reaction should not necessarily be a feeling of rejection. However, no matter the reason, it's not what you're used to. And just remember it could be worse. Brenda told me about the man who asked her to leave *his* place in the middle of the night: " 'It's time you leave. I'll call you a cab,' he said without warning. Shit, I got out of there fast and wondered where my head was at for going in the first place. He got what he wanted and got rid of me. What an awful experience."

Don't forget your options. Did it ever occur to you that in the middle of the night you might feel a wave of anxiety at the prospect of spending the entire night with a man who is not your husband? So don't be surprised to hear yourself saying: "Sorry, but I think it's time for you to leave."

It's perfectly okay. One woman told me: "I had been divorced six months and had been dating an old friend. The first time we had sex was pretty good, considering, but when it was all over I got sick to my stomach. I really started thinking about my marriage and I wanted desperately to be alone. So I asked my friend to leave. Thank God he understood. I told him that I was depressed and was going into a bad head trip.

"Fortunately I could tell him why. He was very understanding. I made some fresh coffee, we talked about his divorce, and he left me to my mood. The next day he called to see if I was okay. He was so nice about it that eventually I was able to look forward to spending the whole night with him. That first time was just too much."

She handled herself well. She told the truth. And her beau understood. Don't expect them all to understand. Some men will whine, complain, and even get angry. Hold your ground. Better he's inconvenienced than you.

There are some cases where it becomes all too clear that you have made a dreadful mistake. That the idea of waking up to this attractive—well, he had been at dinner—man would be more than you could bear. That he really had as much imagination in bed as a fly on roast beef. That he was antagonistic when he couldn't maintain an erection. Well, those same words

166

apply. "I think it's time for you to leave." And don't take no for an answer.

In either case, enjoy the luxury of your freedom of choice. Remember those nights when you would have given your signature scarf to your sworn enemy if your husband would have done a disappearing act after one of those disappointing nights in bed?

The same advice applies when you're at his place. If you don't want to spend the night, don't. Obviously it's easier to plan ahead. If it's been a bad day and you know you want to wake up in your own bed alone and yet you want a few hours with him at his place, tell him up front. That's the easiest way. But sometimes there's no accounting for that desire to get home right in the middle of the night. Occasionally it's apparent you should never have said yes in the first place (you said yes to avoid the loneliness). However, there will be times when you are having a perfectly wonderful evening and then flash: instant suffocation. That feeling is par for the recovery course. Usually it's a feeling of being too much like being married and it's a revolution of feelings about your marriage—angry or sad. Whatever, home is where you want to be. So if you want to leave, go. I have left when:

1. I wanted to change clothes for the office the next day.

2. I felt I needed the security of starting the day from my house.

3. I realized I'd made an awful mistake by saying yes in the first place.

4. I just wanted to be alone (usually from overwhelming desire to give in to an irrational pang of fondness for my ex-husband).

3. Sex Talk

How's this for a mood scene: we are relaxing in the twilight of total satisfaction of lovemaking, dazed by no sleep, and feeling very very warm, naked and pure. We are sipping some wine and smoking cigarettes; we touch each other. Then:

"Am I as good as your husband?"

So much for the romantic mood. And since that time I have heard:

"Is your husband as big as I am (or as small?)"—when I tell him how much I love to touch him.

"Did your husband love your breasts as much as I do?"—as he snuggles in for warmth.

"Did your husband ever tell you you had a beautiful back?"—as he traces his fingers down my spine.

"How could your husband leave a piece of ass like you?"—intended to be a compliment but was an ill-advised comment considering the circumstances; who needed him (ex) at that moment?

"How many men have you slept with since your divorce?"—as he begins to feel insecure.

"How many men did you sleep with before you were married?"—this sudden interest in my past begins to unnerve me.

"Why did your marriage fail—sex?"—implication that I was terrible, or that my husband was worse; answering this fishing expedition could only have led to unnecessary confidences and recriminations.

"Did you cheat on your husband?"—as he starts to formulate plans for our future and wants assurances I'm loyal.

"Was your husband having affairs?"—what's the point? It's none of his business.

I have heard every one of those miserable questions over a period of time with different men. These are my forbidden topics. And they should be for you too. At this point in your life, your sex life is your business (everyone else's idea of your privacy not withstanding), and that goes for the guy you are in bed with too.

Eventually, if any kind of relationship develops between you and a man, some of these questions are only natural in order to understand and get to know you. Even then, it's up to you to decide how much of your past sex life you are going to share with the man. How much detail of intimacy does he have a right to know about? Why is he asking at all? You're the only person who can decide where to draw the line of good taste. Make sure you think before answering.

Until you know the man, the intellectually superior way to answer any questions about your sex life—before, during, and after marriage—is to, and in this order:

1. nod your head sleepily
2. toss your hair over your eyes
3. look dreamy, sexy, and horny as can be (imagined)
4. reach for him

He should by now have forgotten his question altogether—that there was anyone else in your life but him at that moment. And if he still persists, give up. Take a shower—together if you like. And if still he won't give up, ask him why he continues to dwell on it? And if he still persists, give up on him altogether. He's a creep. Curiosity is one thing; most men will ask in one form or another. But morbid pursuit is perverse.

That doesn't mean talking about sex can't be a real turn-on. But keep your ex-husband out of it. There should be other experiences you can relate to turn you both on now. No matter what turns you on, if you violate the marriage bed with details of your sex life, that guy is never going to forget that. If you can talk about your husband, you can say anything . . . and he's never going to trust you not to talk about him. It's altogether different to tell him about a nameless old love and what you used to do to each other; that's not the same; that's not real competition. But when it comes to your husband, some things are inviolate and your sex life with him should be. Good taste creeps up—like an erection. Your husband, for some nameless, inane reason, is semisacrosanct to a lot of men. Their own anxieties about being husbands are seldom so naked.

Male insecurities are unbelievably complicated (as ours are). When fishing for a compliment, when asking you to compare him with your ex, he may never forget that you answered by comparing and he will forget

169

altogether that he *asked* you to compare. If you answer, you don't have a chance as June.

"I had been seeing one guy for a while and we had a really good sex life in bed. One day we were lying there totally relaxed when my ex-husband came up in the conversation. Well, actually the size of men's cocks came up. He asked me what I thought of his. And I told him I thought it was big. He pursued. Bigger than your husband's? No, I answered. Yours is big but my husband's was bigger. This really sounds like an innocent conversation but after three hours of lovemaking, there's no telling what you're going to talk about, is there? Anyway, about three weeks later, when he was feeling moments of insecurity, he hurled all kinds of things at me about how awful I was and then laid it on thick when he said: 'And I don't need you comparing my cock to your husband's!' I could have died. I thought I never had done that, but then I remembered the conversation . . . I should never have been so honest. He never forgot. And in his mind, I was doing the comparing."

She learned her lesson. He never stopped accusing her of comparing him to her husband. That was the end of that love affair. So if it's reassurances he wants, not really details of your married life, give him what he asks for, no more. We all want to hear compliments, and men are no different. Maybe you *have* been withholding, even if it should be apparent that you both have been having one hell of a good time. (I know I never fail to be delighted when a man tells me, in words, about the pleasure we are giving each other. It's an added spice to lovemaking.) Amanda advises:

"If you tell him his cock is gigantic, tastes as yummy as a box of buttered popcorn, and feels like velvet steel inside of you, that should be telling him a lot. If he still persists, then better double check: maybe his insecurities are taking all the fun away."

The joy of having terrific sex after five years of mediocre marriage sex may call for a celebration. But there is no need to make announcements about it.

170

One woman I know couldn't resist. She told her lover that she was more sexually happy with him than ever with her husband. That he was a much better lover and she had thought she was living in a wasteland with her husband. It was forgotten at the time, but something clicked weeks later and her own words were thrown back at her, calculated to hurt. And they did.

"It was the second time we had sex. The first time had been quick but passionate. It was hot; temperatures in the nineties and the air-conditioner was not working. We sat in my living room for a few hours talking, and drinking the coolest drinks we could find. It was pretty funny: we kept taking off our clothes, you know, my shoes, his shoes, his shirt, my top, my slacks, and we made incredible love. Really torrid. The ice cubes fell out of the glass that was lying next to us on the floor. It was a shock to the system when I rolled over on one of them. It was right at the small of my back. He was inside of me and rather than get up I sort of grooved on the sensation. Every time he went deeper, the cold would run through my body. Ice cubes. The new plaything. We got some more and started running them all over each other. Then he took one cube and carressed my cunt with it. It hurt, but no pain. I am not into any pain scene. It was perfectly ridiculous but so refreshing. I sound like a cola commercial . . . but it was. Then he took the ice cube and licked it and then he licked me. It was so good. It was cold and I never felt anything like it. Since my pussy was so warm by now the cube melted. His tongue on the ice, on me. On the ice, on me. It was better than jumping into the ocean when the beach was ninety degrees. Then, as I was about to come, zoop, into my vagina. A whole ice cube. It was heaven. But now the lousy part; about four weeks later, another hot night, and this time the air-conditioning was fixed but I couldn't get out of my mind all these weeks the feeling of that ice cube, cold and wet in my warm soft vagina. We started to make love and I suggested ice cubes. He was in a terrible mood and said no. But the way

171

he said it: 'Why should I have to do that when you said I was better than your husband?' I froze. Oh, I didn't need any pun. I realized he was in a bad mood but he didn't have to throw my lousy sex life with my husband in my face. I should have thrown him out then. But I didn't. We made love. My heart really wasn't in it. And although I continued to see him a few weeks more, I figure that that night was the end."

4. Inexperience Shows

The assumption of experience—sexual—when it comes to the DW is staggering. Just because you've been married everyone expects you to be less phony about sex than the never-married woman (yes, you may) and generally more willing to experiment sexually than a single woman would be. Dr. Paul Gillette feels no remorse in furthering the image of the with-it, know-it-all divorcee. In truth, it's quite different. Most divorced women are terrified at the thought of sex. Oh, they might fancy its delicious aspects but secretly wonder about some of the logistics of the specifics. Dr. Gillette and others would have us believe that the announcement of the DW's entry would read: DIVORCEE AVAILABLE FOR SEX. WILL TRY ANYTHING. GUARANTEED NEVER TO SAY NO. In fact, it should read: DIVORCED WOMAN IN NEED OF LOVING. NEEDS VARIETY. HAS BODY AND IS WILLING TO LEARN.

ASK AND YE SHALL GET

It is important for a woman to ask for what turns her on in bed. This is often a new experience for a DW since she has been having sex with the same man who, hopefully, at least at one time, knew exactly what to do to arouse his partner. Remember when your husband used to give you a sensual massage? And now it seems you just can't find a man who thinks of it as a turn-on—or at any rate acts on it. Do you just wish he'd get with it, or are you doing something about it? It is your responsibility to express your wishes. Don't be so grateful for his attentions that you don't mention what your needs are. And don't fall for the myth that nice girls don't ask. People ask: man or woman. Just as we are expected to indicate our preferences about meat—well-done, medium—we are expected to direct our lovemaking.

Upon entering the world of the newly liberated, you have to work on getting what you want. It really isn't so difficult. And not only will you get what you want, your lover should be turned on to a woman who knows herself well enough to ask for it. He'll also be grateful and when you reach the lovely climax because of his extra care (and your careful guidance), he'll feel that he satisfied you. And it goes without saying that you'll be satisfied, delighted, and feel pretty good yourself.

Lottie, thirty-five, long-legged, and considered sophisticated by her friends, was used to getting what she wanted; however, she was a dummy when it came to lovemaking. She told me that she was into sensual massage with her ex-husband and since her split no man had suggested it despite eight months of looking. Finally she wised up.

"I was seeing a terrific guy at the time. He suggested we go to Antigua for the weekend. I was all ready: two bathsuits, a pair of sandals, two long cotton dresses, suntan lotion, a book on tropical fish, and a bottle of love oil. When we got the hotel, I unpacked and put on the table next to the bed all the books from my luggage. We went to the pool for a dip in the morning and he left to shower before lunch and left me to sun myself a little longer. When I got back to the room, he was there lounging on the terrace, nude, reading the massage book. And he was hard already. I smiled, went and got the oil, took off my bathsuit, and the next three hours were sensational. Cool underneath our wet bathing suits. I lay on the bed stomach down. His warm hands took the oil and meddled into my back, rubbing it ever so gently. All over. By the time he reached my ass, I was a quivering, relaxed woman. And then his hands between my legs. I'm turning myself on by telling the story.. Warm, oily, sexy. Oil all over: breasts, in my cunt, between my legs. And suddenly

173

I came. He was delighted. I could see that. He was as hard as a rock. It was my turn to give him the sensual massage."

All she had to do was ask and she got. So can you. Grace, married five years and then divorced, was appalled because her lover didn't know what she wanted. Wrongly, she felt he should be so in tuned to her needs that he would know.

"Since I never had to tell my husband what I wanted, I just figured that was true love personified. I was just angry if Bill, my current lover, didn't know that I wanted to be on top on a particular night. Finally I just blurted out: 'You're so selfish, you only do what you want.' At which point he told me that I never put in any requests. And he was right. He then asked me what I wanted and I told him. 'Tonight I don't feel like being underneath.' 'So be it.' And we had a terrific time. All I had to do was ask."

Once Grace realized that a lover is not necessarily a mind reader, she had less problems getting satisfaction in bed. And so will you.

And don't forget to ask *for more* if you want it. When you're with a man who turns you on, and you've made love, had breakfast, and you are turned on again, don't hesitate to make your wishes known. Susie had been called oversexed in the last year of her marriage by her husband, who was trying to tell her he didn't want any part of her. She carried this notion right through the divorce and into her first major love affair after the divorce.

"I was so afraid to make any demands because my ex had told me in no uncertain terms that there was something wrong with me. That I wanted too much; that all I cared for was sex sex sex and there were more things to life, etc. So when I started dating after my divorce, I tried to be very careful not to show my needs. It turned out to be a big mistake. After a few months, and a few different men, I still felt I wasn't getting my share of loving. Then I met a man who not only made terrific love, but liked to talk to me about it.

I finally confessed to him there were times I really got turned on but I was afraid to tell him. He made me realize how silly that was. He told me that I could have and should have all that I wanted. It was terrific. Rather than coming with me the first time, he would let me come a few times before he did. This was the way I got what I wanted a hundred percent and he enjoyed making me come so much that he would get even more excited than in the beginning of our relationship."

Not all women are lucky enough to have lovers they can talk to so easily, but all women should be getting exactly what they need—even if they have to look around until they find the right man.

But even if you tell him exactly what you want, maybe you still won't feel satisfied. What turned you on with your husband may not turn you on with your lover. In fact, Linda found out that even if her lover did exactly what her husband did, it didn't mean satisfaction.

"I was having an affair with my dentist and it was like pulling teeth to get what I wanted. I just loved having my cunt tickled by my husband. When I told my lover about it, he carried on like a trouper. But it left me cold. I panicked. Nothing I could do aroused me. I told him to stroke my breasts. But nothing he could do could arouse me either. I finally gave up the affair—I mean, there was no point in continuing it. But I thought it was me. It wasn't until later that I realized it was the dentist. I really didn't like him and nothing he could do could ever make me that passionate."

That's one way to look at it. And don't forget that what you thought was groovy with hubby may be just routine now. Explore different possibilities. In fact, try his way for a change.

TRY IT HIS WAY FOR A CHANGE

It doesn't matter if your husband was as innovative as "M," the sensuous man, or if he had as much imagination as King Kong courting Fay Wray. If it was great or boring, when you were married there were just the two of you—each contributing your own input to the sexual playground. Now that you are no longer married you have the chance to see what other amusements are for your pleasure. It doesn't matter what or who you are: if you were a virgin when you married, or an experienced twenty-five-year-old, there is always something new to learn about your body and what it responds to.

There's rarely anything as discouraging as a closed mind. My friend, Dorothy, is a good example. "Look, I know what I like and that's the only way," she said to me recently. She had been separated six months and we were having lunch to mark the day the divorce became final. She had been married eight years to a stockbroker. I also knew her sexual needs were not being neglected. I felt quite confident about talking to her for material when I was writing this book. When I asked her if she had tried having sex in any new ways since her divorce she told me her routine: "I suck him for a few minutes, he jiggles my clit, and then gets on top of me and goes inside. I put my legs around his and my arms around his neck. If he moves slowly and forcefully, and I move faster, I usually come in a matter of moments. Any other way, any more time spent doing anything else is plain stupid and a waste of time. I always come if I do it right—like I just told you."

Despite my pleas that she was missing out on a lot of fun, that there were a lot of very nice ways to get to the same point and the variety itself was fun, fell on deaf ears. She will go along in her ways, marry a guy who follows a pattern, and will say to herself she is a fulfilled woman. What a waste.

Rochelle, however, was a more adventurous person when it came to her education.

"My husband and I always thought we were totally uninhibited in bed. He was a few years older than I was and he taught me an awful lot. Most of my views, granted, were his. Then when we finally decided to divorce, the bastard had the nerve to tell me that I wasn't adventurous enough in bed. What a blow. That was the first time he actually let on to me (probably not to his mistress) that there was anything bothering him about our sex life. If he had only told me, I'm sure I could have come up with a few winners (after all, I wasn't exactly a virgin when I married him). But that leads me to the second point: he always took the lead. I couldn't even suggest his favorites. He had to be the one to decide what we would do any given night. It may have been interesting and there may have been variety, but it was his show all the way. After we got divorced, I saw no reason not to sleep with as many men as possible. I learned all kinds of new ways to excite, arouse, and delight a man. And I found that I was aroused in all kinds of ways. One day I counted. I learned eleven different ways to have intercourse in six months. Last year I remarried. And my husband loves me in bed. Our king-sized bed is the pleasure palace on those long Saturday afternoons. Not only does he love it when I try something new, but he has a lot more to look forward to. It's fantastic to be with a man who treats you as an equal in the bed."

In order to get the most from your new freedom, throw out the old prejudices. Be open to guidance and suggestion. Above all, don't get hung up on the following notions:

"I always hated that . . ."

"I thought it was dirty . . ."

"Well, I've never done that before because . . ."

Jennifer, a twenty-five-year-old DW with two children and a two-year marriage that went bad, found out that what she hated with her husband was an altogether different story with her new lover, Oliver.

"I couldn't stand it when my husband ate me. I always hated that. I let him at first, but he could tell it really wasn't getting to me. There were lots of other things that did turn me on so he relied on those, I

177

guess. Eventually he didn't even bother and I was really deep down relieved. I could never understand what the point was . . . what any woman got out of it. And I thought that was me . . . we all had different turn-ons, right? And I thought I knew me. I got divorced and started dating. I really got interested in this one guy, Oliver. It just seemed natural at one point during sex that he started to move his head right into my pussy. I must have started because he put his hand firmly but gently on my stomach. I relaxed. He licked my pussy wet all over and it felt nice. Nothing really exciting. His tongue started flashing with more energy and into my vagina; outside and inside. I realized later that I really liked it. I didn't come but I was getting used to it. It really felt good. Four nights later, I came with Oliver's tongue licking my pussy. I really can't tell you how he differed from my husband. But somehow the reaction was altogether different. Now I love it."

If Jennifer had said no to Oliver because it never turned her on, she would have missed one of the finer pleasures in life and an added yummy to her sex life.

Liz, thirty-six years old, red-haired, married five years, divorced six months, revised her whole attitude about talking about sex. She felt some words were dirty and shouldn't be said while making love. Then she met Jake.

"Okay, I'll tell you what happened to me. It's perfectly clear that fuck, cunt, pussy, cock are merely words. I had read them, heard them, and even used them. I really wasn't a prude. But I just couldn't see the turn-on when you were in bed. Before I was married, I was seeing one guy who loved to talk about my pussy and I thought he was vulgar and crude. Then I got married, and about a year into the marriage my husband, in one of his inventive moods, said something like: 'I'm going to put my big cock into your wet pussy and fuck you.' He said it while we were making love and I couldn't believe my ears. Who the hell did he think I was anyway. It was the first and last time he ever got verbal in bed. My tears showed him exactly

178

how I felt. Dirty. My next experience was altogether different. By then I was divorced and taking a vacation from worries. I got myself very involved with sailing. Something I had given up altogether when I was married. I had a sailfish and would go out a few times a week. I was taking a two-year degree in psychiatric social work so I had some free mornings. There was a man at the marina who also seemed to have a lot of free time. After a week of eyeing each other we finally said hello and from there conversation about sailing was about it for another week. Then one day this man turned to me in the midst of discussing the wind direction and said: 'Tonight, Liz, I am going to eat your pussy.' I couldn't believe my ears. Not because he was interested in me sexually. We both knew our friendship was leading up to that. But the words actually turned me on. I shuddered with expectation and for some reason it was the sexiest thing I had ever heard. Go figure it. Sex with him was dynamite. He kept up a running pattern of enticements, threats, and demands in the most erotic language possible. And I'll confess it was contagious. I learned a few new sweet murmurings for his ears only. What was once awful and disgusting was music to my ears with this man. I really learned that talking while making love could be a real gas."

Which would you rather hear: "You have a warm juicy genital area?" or "You have a warm, juicy pussy?"

I'VE NEVER DONE THAT BEFORE BECAUSE . . .

If a man asks you to do something in bed you can always say no if you don't want to do it. You are not on call—that's what prostitutes are for. Even a high-priced girl can't afford to say no—that's what she's paid for. Once committed to spend the night with a man, she's his property. Not so you. Just because he has paid for your dinner, you can still say no at the door *and* in bed. Not only is it your right, it is an obligation to yourself. But if you find yourself saying a lot of no's because you've never done that before, reconsider.

179

Are you in a rut? Are you acting on old prejudices? Are you still judging sex as good or bad, clean or dirty? You should "no" better. Nothing is dirty or bad when you and your lover are enjoying yourself.

Many women I talked to were eager to tell me about their education and how certain rigid notions were discarded when they realized what liberated really meant.

Debra tried something new. She may never do it again, but it was something she'll never forget.

"I'll tell you something that happened to me. Me, Demure Debra, my husband used to call me. Our wedding night was the first for me. My husband used to be pretty uptight about sex, I realize that now. And I was so uptight, I didn't even realize he was. But secretly I was curious about how other people did it. Once I said this to him and he got red in the face and we had an argument that lasted for three days. He had some stake in keeping me virginal.

"Fortunately we got divorced. The funny thing is, he did it. And I was upset, but not that upset. I wouldn't admit it then, but I will now. I wanted to do those things I heard other people did.

"So I did. And when David came home—he was a guy I had been seeing for a month—with a video tape machine, it wasn't for tapes of me cooking chicken dinner. He brought it into the bedroom and set it up so we could take movies of ourselves fucking. I was silent as we set it up. But I didn't say no. He had a sixteen-millimeter camera set up on a tripod in his bedroom. At first I was a little inhibited but then I really got into the sex and forgot about the camera. The next time I saw him, we projected the whole film of us, the two of us, making it. And it was such a groove, we made love during the movie. It was a weird sensation. There I was on the wall sucking his cock and here I was on the bed with him inside of me. Just the thought and realization sent off a barrage of sensations and I had an orgasm like I never had before.

180

We did it a few times and then lost interest. But I can thank him for one of the most incredible experiences of my life. I learned there's no harm in trying new turn-ons."

If Debra had said no because she had never done "that" before, she would have been the loser.

Laura, through experience and an intelligent inquisitive mind, changed her mind about using the vibrator in her lovemaking. Having been married for thirteen years, she was virtually a virgin when she was on her honeymoon. Once divorced, her views on sex came from her marriage—and using a vibrator was not included.

"The first time a man brought the vibrator to bed with us I thought he was stark raving mad and that I had found my way into a bizarre sexual fantasy of a sexual pervert. I quietly said I didn't like it and froze inside. About two months later I encountered the vibrator again. How many sexual crazies can you meet in a year? Maybe I had the wrong idea. The tickling sensation rubbing the inside of my thighs, the steady force on my clit, the vagina, was getting to me. But I still couldn't really relax. You know, I had seen ads for the vibrator. I guess they usually come in the size of a full penis; battery controlled, the whole works. The funny thing is I had heard a lot of jokes about it—usually in reference to a woman masturbating. The old banana snicker had turned into the vibrator joke. And I also heard tales from girl friends who had gone to Europe and wound up in bed with Frenchmen who came equipped with this little added attraction. The point is I never figured it would arrive in my bed. But once I got over the idea of the mechanical vibrator, I just decided to enjoy it."

And she did.

Joan had been married for three years and when she got divorced felt that there was only one way to have sex: with the man on top.

"My husband was older than I was and I just figured he was more experienced. During my marriage the topic of sex rarely was discussed. When it was, my husband made his views clear. Any positions other than the traditional were, according to him: 'for acrobats, animals, and hippies.' It just isn't natural, he told me when I had the nerve to question him about it later. But he had me convinced. After all, that same judgmental attitude pervaded my life. Always pronouncements about wrong or right whenever I did anything. Needless to say, it began to drive me stark raving mad. I went back to school and there I realized that I wasn't crazy. That people accepted me for me. Lots of other things too. But we finally got divorced. And I had no problem finding men to sleep with me. Lots of darling lovers around the school. Invariably I found myself in bed. And then, once, on top. I was ready to send for the riot squad. My quick response to hysteria broke up that romance. But then it happened so many times in the next few months that I began to wonder about me. I went out and bought three books on sex. It only verified what I found out. It was perfectly normal. And what's more, as a woman on top I could dig sex even more. It was a difficult transition to make. I really didn't know where to put my legs. But eventually I made it. I can really dig it; I mount him and move like there's no tomorrow. My husband really did a number on me, didn't he?"

I couldn't agree more.

Joy told me, "My husband hated to have me suck him off so I thought most men felt that way. He told me that he thought it was something that only perverts liked. And since he was the only man I ever slept with, how would I know the difference? It was only after getting the divorce, sleeping with a few different men, that I realized that men do like to be eaten as much as I do."

Susanna told me that there were things that she

never realized "in a million years a man would like. I mean, it just didn't occur to me to swallow his semen when I brought him off in my mouth. It just never crossed my mind that a man would find that exciting. Fortunately, about six months after my divorce I started seeing a man who was very definite in his likes and dislikes. He practically told me exactly how to turn him on. I didn't complain. He was one hell of a terrific lover. Finally, after a week or so, he asked me to swallow his semen when he came as I was sucking him. I thought he was kidding. Usually just when he would reach the bursting point I would push him gently away. Then one night it was different. He held my head on his cock and shouted: 'Swallow it.' And I did. And his pleasure was incredible. It was different than before. I just never thought a man would like it. My husband never mentioned it; in fact, he would push my head away just before he came. So I thought that was the way it was. I was wrong, wrong. And you know, I enjoyed even more knowing that his come was inside me."

The moral is: Don't let old habits and turn-offs keep your sex life in a boring pattern. There is more than one route to satisfaction.

5. No Orgasm . . . How Come?

The orgasm has emerged from low profile to one of the hottest topics of any sexual dialogue. That it is one of the areas of physical as well as psychological tensions obviously contributes to much of the controversy. Despite the attention, experts can't seem to agree on the nature of orgasm: clitoral vs. vaginal orgasm (are they the same? physically? mentally?) the multiple orgasm (the answer for all women?) mutual orgasm (the highest pleasure? see *Ideal Marriage*).

While I don't pretend to enter the melee of discussion with special credentials, I do intend to give my personal opinion on this matter where it particularly relates to the DW. That is, many women have complained that for the first time in their lives they are sexually frustrated—after divorce.*

Before discussing the nonorgasmic encounter, I'd like to analyze the question: What is orgasm? Hopefully, if you understand the question, you may well be on the road to having them again.

Dr. Reuben, in *Everything You Always Wanted to Know About Sex,* skirts the issue by heading a section on orgasm "WHAT HAPPENS DURING ORGASM?" (pp. 42–44). While seeming to paraphrase in popular terms what Masters and Johnson wrote in specific scientific terms, he really doesn't answer the question: "Transmission lines and circuits of the entire body are suddenly and deliciously overloaded. The wires get red-hot, the fuses blow, the bells chime—and then it's all over until the next time." Can you relate to that?

Meanwhile, the king and queen of sexual research and therapy, Masters and Johnson, are more exacting, but generally less accessible: they give three interacting factors that work on a woman during a sexual experience aimed toward orgasm: (1) "physiologic (characteristic physical conditions and reactions during the peak of sex tension increment); (2) psychologic (psychosexual orientation and receptivity to orgasmic attainment; and (3) sociologic (cultural, environmental, and social factors influencing orgasmic incidence or ability)." (p. 127, *Human Sexual Response.*)

In other words, (1) you have to be turned on to the man in a physical way and be stimulated physically; (2) you have to be in the right frame of mind to even receive this stimulation, and (3) outside factors have to be eliminated so you're not too uptight to function.

That doesn't answer the question: what is orgasm? But it sure does tell us a lot about why some women

*For those women who have never achieved any kind of orgasm (by masturbating, coitus, or manipulation by your partner) I suggest seeking professional help. Therapy is what you need. It needn't be the most expensive sex clinics, either. A professional psychotherapist no doubt will help you.

have complained about not having orgasm with men after the divorce or separation. Further:

"An overview of female sexual dysfunction commonly reveals a stalemate in the sociosexual adaptive process at the point which a woman's desire for sexual expression crashes into personal fear or conviction that her role as a sexual entity is without the unique contribution of herself as an individual. For some reason . . . her confidence in herself as a functional sexual entity has been impaired." (p. 315, *Human Sexual Inadequacy*.)

And that's it, isn't it?

Just think: "Her confidence in herself as a functional sexual entity has been impaired." It is logical then to figure out what the reason is: that of a busted marriage, for starters. That of a lousy sex life with your husband, especially as your miserable life together was extended into the bedroom. So right after divorce, if you lose the ability for orgasm, don't think your life has been ruined. It's time to build up your image of yourself as a functional sexual woman. If you feel good about yourself, and really believe it, you have a better chance to have the orgasm. And even if you think you feel pretty terrific, just remember that there is an unconscious possibility working overtime that is sending doubts to your brain.

Masters and Johnson continue: "The blocking of receptivity to sexual stimuli is an unfortunate result of factors which deprive her of the capacity to value the sexual component of her personality or prevent her from placing its value within the context of her life." So think about that. What it's trying to say to you is that in order to respond to sexual stimuli you have to be a together receiving force willing to accept and value the sexual aspect of who you are, and know where it belongs in your life.

Therefore, if you are scared, feel your husband thought you were awful in bed (and therefore, so must all men), feel guilty about having sex with someone you are not married to (and watch out for this one, it still hangs around spooking the life out of DW's I

185

know, especially in those early months), don't get paranoid about it.

Even Dr. Reuben relates to why some women don't reach orgasm. "Sex plus fear means no orgasm. Sex plus guilt means no orgasm." And he's on the right track. If you aren't totally relaxed and you are ambivalent about the whole encounter (I want to, but I shouldn't because . . . ; or I want to, but I'm scared to death . . .) the likelihood of attaining orgasm is small.

So, from these and other sources, I have devised my own notion of orgasm. Perhaps by sharing it with you it might help you regain the lost orgasm.

Orgasm is the state of losing control. All control. Of letting the sensations of being touched (and of touching) be primary. Participation in the sexual act(s) by responding freely allows the tensions to build with pleasure—and finally with total abandonment feel the release. And that is orgasm.

So even if the spirit is willing and the lover is the greatest, factors, real or fancied, are working on you to block your free and liberated response. It is not surprising then that when a divorced woman ventures into the world she finds trouble in giving herself over to enjoyment. There are a thousand and one things that provide blocks: lousy self-image, guilt about non-marital sex, anxiety about his being satisfied with you (or you with him). Any and all things—real or imagined—could be working overtime—conscious or unconscious—when you finally are in bed with a man.

If you do manage to have orgasm the first time, then great. You've got nothing to worry about.

If you don't have orgasm the first time, then you still don't have anything to worry about. But you may have something to work on.

It's time for you to gradually understand the rhythms of your body responding once again and thereby re-establishing your sexual identity as an independent woman. Gratification should naturally follow.

IX.

The Ball's in Your Court

1. Your Vacation

Take this time as an opportunity to make new friends, feel uninhibited by familiar surroundings, and hopefully make the most of the possibilities for romanticism and passion. More bluntly, go where the men are. And more wisely, stay away from that honeymoon spot.

Get out of town. Leave the kids with your mother. Go. Alone or with a girlfriend. There are all kinds of trips: we see them advertised every day. The gourmet trip; the theater trip; the sun-and-sunshine trip; travel by rail or by air. Whatever your choice or inclination, make sure it is a place where you can relax—be yourself—and where there are other unattached people. It's a sexy sojourn you're looking for so make sure you don't fall into the trap of:

• going to the resort in the mountains that caters to couples and families

• returning to the old-standby spot where you and your ex tried the second honeymoon

• traveling with your mother to the Greek Islands

even if she promises to pick up all your luxury expenses

● traveling cross-country with three female friends in one small car

● visiting your sister and brother-in-law who feel your divorce is the end of the world.

Here's some advice from fellow-travelers:

Liz: "Don't go any place that will bring up memories of your husband. Do go where you can experiment with the discovery of yourself."

Suzanne: "Go to Europe if you can swing it. There's nothing like a foreign language to make you forget the loneliness of your life."

Dorothy: "Travel light. You never know when you're going to want to make a side trip with the fabulous stranger you happened to meet at the track in Caracas."

Linda: "Go to a resort that is known for its mobility. And of the islands in the Caribbean, find hotels that cater to the single person—or divorced. Off-season is really cheap too."

Sandra: "If you choose the right place your phone will be ringing when you get home. I went to the Club Med in Martinique and the informal atmosphere relaxed me so much I really had a good time. And I felt good about myself for the first time in ages. When I got home, there was more than one phone call from men I had met down there. My social life really began. All I needed was a chance to get away from the burden of divorce and children for my old self to come out."

Cassandra went into great detail when I asked her about her post-divorce period and vacations:

"When Hank and I split up and I realized that I was alone and I got that telegram from Mexico telling me that for sure, and once and for all we were no longer

188

married, I was beside myself. I looked in the mirror. Despite the circles under my eyes from crying, I saw an attractive, dark-haired—long—woman with a sexy ass (how many men had told me that) but I really couldn't believe that I could get unnumb to be turned on by any man. I looked around our bedroom. It all of a sudden had become my bedroom and I felt I was going to suffocate from loneliness. I just cried myself to sleep that night.

"Fortunately I had a job. So the next day I went to work like nothing had happened. I kept glancing at myself in the reflection of the mirror. No one else knew what I knew. I was no longer married. I also was wishing that I knew someone to make it with. You know, to kiss my breasts, to eat me . . . well, you said to be honest . . . to put his penis inside of me and to pump and pump and pump. Then—oh, well . . . I looked around and everyone reminded me of my husband. I just couldn't seem to find anyone that interested me. Sure, I had lots of offers. Who doesn't when she announces she is divorced? Then, and you won't believe this, I saw a movie on television—I watched a lot of TV those days—where a girl meets this marvelous man on a plane as they are flying across the country. That night I dreamed about taking a trip and the next day I found myself wandering into the travel agency and I walked out with all kinds of folders. To make a long story short, I went into my boss at work and told him that I had two weeks' vacation coming and since I was getting over the trauma of divorce could I please have an extra two weeks. He was agreeable. So within two weeks I was packed and ready to go and, you know, I knew why I was going. I mean at the airport I just began to vibrate and send out the clues . . . I really believe in that, don't you? . . . and I was sitting there waiting for the flight to be called and a man came and sat next to me. He asked me why I was going to Paris . . . I'd picked that as my first stop. I planned to go there and then on the train to Greece, with a stopover in Rome. I never made it to Rome, but that's getting ahead of my story. Well, I started on the plane and

189

literally fucked my way all over Europe. Okay, I know you want me to be specific so here goes:

"Luck must have been with me. You know the computer sets up who you are going to sit with and I found myself next to a man who was very busy with his papers even before the flight took off. He didn't even look up . . . no, that's not true . . . he did look up when I stepped on his foot trying to get into my window seat; he looked up with annoyance. However, when they brought the drinks around he put down his papers and turned to me with a dazzling smile and I almost died, having given up on him long before then; just about when the seat belt signs went off. Anyway, he smiled and asked if he could buy me a drink. I nodded assent, gave my order, and we began to chat. Before I knew it I was telling him all about my marriage and that I was scared to death because I was traveling alone and that I was really excited because I had never been to Paris. And this you won't believe. He went to Paris often, even spoke French, and invited me for dinner the second night we were there. Dinner, and yes, we went back to his hotel and since he knew that I was divorced and that I had really been starved for sex since before my marriage broke up, he was really kind. Oh, it was beautiful. We had an elegant dinner, and he kissed me a number of times, just brushed his lips on my hair as we got into the taxi, my fingers as he helped me up to go to the ladies' room. We had wine and laughed a lot. Then we were in his room. I became very embarrassed. He knew it. He continued to talk and to be very gentle. More wine and more talk. He caressed more softly and gently. I couldn't believe it. I was in Paris and here was this marvelous man saying beautiful things to me. We got undressed in the semidarkness and he just held me to him unclothed. The joy of that. Then he started to move his warm hand up and down my arms, my legs, my breasts, my stomach, between my legs. It was my night and he was giving it to me. I knew it and relaxed. I was getting wetter and wetter between my legs and then just as instinct I began to caress him. Finally I wanted

190

him to be inside me. He was big and erect and slipped right inside of my vagina and you know, and I wouldn't have believed this, I came. I just came right then and there. Then he came and we just fell into each other's arms. I remember him just talking to me, gently. It was fantastic. We made love in so many different positions that night that I can't even remember them all. I loved every minute of it. I was alive again. The next day I went back to my hotel and got my things and moved in with him. Yes, I knew he had a wife in the States and I knew he would be in Paris for only four more days. But those four days were the most important four days in my life. He made me feel. He made me give and take with a man. He showed me things I would never have tried with any other man. We had anal sex, we sat naked and played word games, we made love in the bathtub. Then he left and I was wandering around Paris without him. I felt an acute sense of loss. And I knew I would never see him again. I couldn't. It had been perfect, those five days, and nothing like it could ever happen again.

"The next day—my last day in Paris—I did manage to find a Parisian. He spoke no English, I spoke no French. But I certainly didn't need a translator to know what he wanted. So I went. Frankly, it wasn't so good but it was interesting. This Frenchman loved to use the vibrator. To be honest with you I had never been turned on by a vibrator before. Oh, I thought it was something that only perverts used. It was interesting. Somehow it didn't get me all turned on. But it was my second experience and I was beginning to enjoy my independence. I would never forget those five days, but I wasn't going to dwell on them either.

"That afternoon I boarded the train, the Orient Express, to take me to Greece. It was some trip. The train in France was new and there were couchettes; those boards that are stacked up three to a side where you can sleep. And sleep I did. The next day we were in Yugoslavia. And the train got rid of those 'luxurious cars.' We were now traveling behind-the-Iron-Curtain style. In the first-class coach . . . and there are only

191

coaches on the train. At first there were six people in the compartment. And it was crowded but my seatmates were friendly. They could speak no English and I no Yugoslavian. But we shared our food—there was no dining car on this train. Then all of them got off except for one man. He was going on to the last stop in Yugoslavia. Every time we stopped at a town the conductor would come in and look at the passports and at the tickets. Well, it was very cold and needless to say, there was this warm-bodied hunk over there on the other side of the compartment. Finally the time came when we looked at each other and shrugged. I got up from my side—he would never make the first move— and got in next to him and he held me. Probably the first capitalist he ever held. I touched his cock only to find it was already erect. I smelled his heavy wool jacket and somehow the whole scene merged and the fantasy became reality and I got so turned on. His hand went right between my legs and you could hear him grunt appreciatively when he felt my wet pussy. I never will know how it was done to this day but somehow my slacks came down to my knees, my pants went down that far, his penis was out and we fucked and fucked and I came and came. That was about all we had time for. I went back to my side of the compartment, exhausted and warm, and when I woke up he was gone. We obviously had stopped in a town and he'd gotten off. I will never figure out to this day why the conductor didn't come to see my ticket and passport. Probably had some kind of sixth sense. I wound up in Athens exhausted and dirty; it had been a thirty-six-hour train ride, no showers, little food, and one torrid love-sex. I went directly to the hotel and took one long hot bath and slept through to the next day. I went around Athens and I was approached for all kinds of things: money, hand-outs, sex, buy, buy, buy and give, give, give. I just wasn't into it and decided to take a car to Delphi. There I met a wonderful man who had taken the bus to Delphi. I offered him a ride back to Athens. While we were talking he said that he was taking a cruise to various islands. He was most enthusiastic. He invited me to dinner. I went. We went back to my room that night and made love. It wasn't all that good but he was funny and bright and kind. He asked me to join him on the cruise. I did. And I had a marvelous week going from island to island, from ruin to ruin. And every night we made love and every afternoon at siesta time we had sex. And it got better and better. He was an American who lived in Switzerland . . . and was touring himself. I was supposed to get to Rome but he convinced me to stay in Greece a little longer. I did willingly . . . when he took me to the airport he said he would find me when he came to New York. We still write and I know I will see him when he gets here and someday I may take another trip to Europe and go to Switzerland to see him. Anyway, I returned and went back to the office and everyone remarked how terrific I looked. Little did they know that I had been on the Sex Tour. It was fantastic. I recommend it to anyone who can afford it. Really do. Changed my whole attitude. And I'm not afraid of men anymore. And I am going out more and more here at home. Really worth every cent. . . ."

I agree with her. Don't you?

Georgina had a social life after her divorce but couldn't really enjoy it. It took a holiday for her to feel relaxed enough to get complete satisfaction.

"I was married for seven years. When we were first married I just couldn't seem to get enough of my husband. And fortunately he of me. We must have fucked everywhere any time we got a chance. It was ridiculous. We were living together at the time so it's not like we had to sneak around. We just sort of couldn't keep our hands off each other and seemed to take great pleasure in balling our heads off wherever we went. After a while all good things come to an end. I won't go through the dismal details of the seven years, just let me say that at the end of the seven years we were each sleeping at the opposite ends of a king-sized bed. When the divorce became final I gingerly started seeing men. I was fascinated with the prospect of renewing those old feelings I'd had with my husband when I first knew him. I reasoned, if I had them once I could have them again. But, and this is the depressing part, I must have slept with, fucked, balled, screwed, whatever you want to call it, with a dozen men. I just couldn't work up a sweat. I felt my body was dead from the vagina down. I was really getting worried. I never had figured myself one of those women magazines are always screaming their headlines to: '10 NEW WAYS, TRIED AND TRUE, FOR YOU TO FINALLY GET YOUR ORGASM,' or 'YOU MEAN YOU NEVER HAVE. . . .'

So I decided to take a trip. To Nassau. Alone. I arrived late and went straight to bed. I was really tired from the plane trip. The next day I went to the beach and the sun was perfect. There were a few clouds but . . . well . . . perfect. I lay in the sun getting very warm and perspirey. My nipples were so erect you could see them through my bathing suit. That sun was turning me on. I wasn't dead, after all. But I wondered if I could keep it up faced with the naked body of a male other than my husband seven years ago. Feeling flushed, having gotten a red nose and a healthy look, I dressed for dinner and decided to go to the casino. I walked into the dining room and ate alone. I had one glass of wine, which made me feel very sultry. A real woman. Then as I was leaving the dining room one of my earrings fell off. I looked under the table and looked up into the bluest eyes I have ever seen in my life. He had longish hair, blond. I looked again. He was tall, very tall, and was dressed in that casual way that I really like. He found my earring and I found my clitoris sending all kinds of messages to my body. I'm sure he heard them because within moments we were sitting next to each other at the blackjack table recklessly losing all the money he had already won. It was with total abandonment that I returned to his room with him. Oh, it was good. He just touched me and I trembled. He moved his hands around to feel my body. When I responded—and hallelujah, I was—he would spend some time stroking and kissing. He learned me very well for the moments we had together. Wet between my legs and ready for him, he went inside of me and . . . I felt a state of incredible warmth . . . well, I can only remember moving against him and him moving inside me. I knew that I would make it. I did. Seven times before we finally emerged the next morning for a late lunch."

Georgina and her lover spent the next two days together. Both returned home—she to New York, he to Cleveland—with promises to keep in touch. It really never worked out. When he came into New York, they tentatively had lunch and they both tactfully agreed that the special something just wasn't there. But nonetheless, Georgina will always have fond memories and a certain gratefulness to the man whom she considered responsible for giving her a new lease on life. All she needed was the attention, and the atmosphere, to clear up old memories and problems.

2. Variety Is . . .

The divorced woman faces a time of limbo, of pain, and of sadness. However, it is also a time for experimentation . . . new lifestyles and a variety of men. There is no time like the present to find out the kind of man that suits you—the new you.

Don't get hung up on "No thanks, he's not my type." After spending some years in a marriage, you may have convinced yourself that your husband was your type (then again, it may be the opposite). Not true. Try this. With a pad and paper, jot down certain characteristics of your ex. What kind of person was he? What were his interests? Not just generalities but specifics. Have you put down the one item in the world you knew your husband would have liked for his next birthday? The kind of shirts he liked to wear? His hobbies? His phobias? What did he do with his "own" time? Did he like to travel? Stay at home while you traveled? Did you ever go out to dinner? His favorite food? What kind of friends did he have? Did he have a lot of acquaintances? The possibilities of a list could be endless. Keep going.

Now, then, look at the list and consider the opposites. This exercise should enable you to see the pattern and, if possible, break it. Now, with an open mind, you might consider accepting a date even if you've heard yourself say to your best friend, "He's not my type."

For example:

If your husband was an intellectual, go out with the onions-and-garlic type. He may have a whole new way in bed and you may not have to listen to the philosophical reasoning of Plato to get there. You may even like Plato, but you may like the new seasonings better.

If your husband was rich, go out with someone who is struggling. It may do you good to have a spaghetti dinner.

If your husband was the silent type, go out with the gabber. It may be a welcome relief not to have to carry the ball of conversation—continuously.

If your husband was a book freak, go out with the guy who resists reading books on the grounds that he read one, once. It may not be the most stimulating conversation but there are other things in life to appreciate.

If your husband was all for equal rights for women, go out with a male chauvinist. Bobby did and she found out that her anger was no longer toward her husband, but to men in general. A healthy transference.

If your husband was a peacock, look for a blue shirt. Sandra's husband, Chris, was always dressed in the most divine clothes: Cardin, Gucci, Blass. When she arrived at a party with him, Sandra found herself alone while everyone, male and female, was gathered around her husband admiring his latest buckle. Her ego suffered. When she and her husband split, she couldn't bear to be with a man who spent a lot of time on his wardrobe.

"I simply didn't have the strength to admire a man's clothes. And I refused to tolerate that vanity. It was such a relief when I started dating Bill. He dressed like a human being. I remember thinking one Sunday when he arrived to go to the zoo with the kids: thank God he's wearing levis, a blue work shirt, and an ordinary Levi jacket. I just could see the headlines in *Women's Wear Daily* if it had been Chris. To the Zoo, Suedes and Leathers.

If your husband was In, find a man who's Out. If he was always "in," with the latest book under his arm (even if he never had read it), or the latest quote in his head, or he thinks it's really "in" to recycle his car every year, or he reads the sports pages (for the gossip!) you may find it a total delight to be with someone who has no idea what other people are doing or are saying and cares even less what the Joneses are buying. He may just care about what he is doing with you.

If your husband was famous, go out with an unknown. If you were constantly being watched by the watchers of the famous, then you owe it to yourself to go out with a total unknown so he can concentrate on you and you alone. This may seem like an example that applies to few women, but many men are well-known in their own town even if their claim to fame is of local import.

Sally was married to a compulsive philanthropist—president of this, chairman of that, volunteer for that. It was great for the town and lousy for the marriage. She recently said to me: "From the day we were married to the day we were divorced, we couldn't spend a quiet evening at home without the phone ringing a dozen times, or go to the restaurant without having people join us at the table. I didn't marry a man, I married the core of every organization and committee in town. Too much."

Sally's aim then was to start looking for men who were a little less eager to be public property.

If your husband came from a large family, find an orphan. This is an exaggeration, of course, but I thought of it after talking to Suzanne. She had been married to Jack for five years and finally they got divorced when she realized her affair with George was getting serious. Needless to say, after the divorce, George became less attractive. But she did tell me about one thing that had attracted her to George. "Jack had this huge family. And he felt that any

197

activity was a failure with less than a zillion people around to participate. That meant his birthday (when I would have preferred a romantic dinner for two), my birthday, when we could have used some time with a few close friends. And he even planned vacations with a cast of thousands. George, on the other hand, was strictly a loner. It was always the two of us. I thought that's what I wanted. In fact, I realize now that what I wanted was somewhere in the middle."

If your husband was cynical and droll, go out with an idealist. Let Charlotte tell it: "My husband, or ex, now, was wry and witty. But he was a cynic. After we divorced, after three years of marriage, every time I met someone who had his humor and pessimistic outlook on life, I would compare him to my husband. Then I decided to change all that. I met an optimist, and idealist, at a party. And although I realized that he was a little too 'let's look on the good side,' I wanted to see what it was like. It was fantastic. He always could cheer me up, he always gave people a chance, and he was truly a beautiful person. I am glad that I pursued him because it got the taste out of my mouth that all men were joyless; after all, I had known one man for three years in the shall we say carnal way, and it soured me until I met my idealist."

If your husband was compulsive, go out with the creative. Susan, who was married to a doctor, found total relief when she started dating again. "My husband was compulsive, serious, and clinical. All good traits to be sure, for a doctor, but you try living with that for a while. There's no fancy, no spontaneity. Everything was planned; everything we did had its, well, procedure, as if we were living in an operating room. Can you imagine what sex is like with Mr. Precision? He had everything timed. I became so fascinated with his schedule, I would concentrate on the digital clock next to the bed and ignore what was going on. That was not only bad sex but it was worse: I used to watch the digital clock next to the bed in order to catch him deviating from schedule: it seemed like it was five minutes to the clit, 6 minutes to the tit, and then penetrate. It really wasn't like that but it seemed that way to me. So when I started going out again, and realized that there were creative types around who never knew where they were going to eat dinner, what positions they were going to have the most fun in bed with that night, I discovered a whole new world. And I loved it."

The guy who reminds you of your ex—can be trouble. This is playing with dynamite. But if you can stand the heat, have fun in the kitchen. And if you wake up in the morning with tears in your eyes rather than stars, don't say I didn't warn you.

We are all attracted to the same type over and over. Sometimes it's just habit. If you can't break the habit then at least be prepared for the consequences. If he looks like your husband, is in the same business as your husband, talks like your husband, you are in for an evening of melancholy rather than ecstasy.

I guess we all have to go through with it to see what it is like. And certainly if a guy turns you on, I wouldn't turn him off just because he reminds you of your husband. But, no doubt, that is why he is turning you on in the first place.

Maybe the blond, bookish type (your ex) is the guy who turns you on. Maybe you are into the trip of fantasizing that it is your husband who has your head on his shoulder. But don't be surprised if in the middle of the night your mind starts playing tricks on you.

Bea said it all: "There we were, really digging sex. I hadn't realized it, but Al looked just like my ex-husband. He was dark-haired, very thin, and moved in a frenetic way. I was turned on all evening. Wow! I just couldn't wait till we got home. I even thought to myself: he reminds me of Joe (that's my husband). Well, I reasoned to myself, Joe used to get me all excited so it was natural I would feel that way about Al. We went to his apartment—and now I realize I should be grateful it wasn't mine—and took a shower together. We dried each other off with big towels and just stood there grinning and touching each other. I was feeling really good. Then we got into bed. He was kissing my breast when I looked down and saw the dark head of hair. For a minute, I know this sounds funny, but for a minute I couldn't remember where I was. That head of hair looked just like my husband's. I literally froze. I was finished for the night. My date never knew why. Next time I went out I stayed away from dark-haired men. Finally that feeling went away but it was a good six months before I'd try it again."

Leslie couldn't wait to get into bed with any look-alike who came along. By attempting to replace her husband with a reasonable facsimile, she never let a relationship develop. She just transferred all of her feelings (bad and good) toward her husband onto a new innocent bystander. Finally she went for professional help in order to understand her miserable experiences in dating and lovemaking. All possible relationships ended rather abruptly—evidently the man realized she really wasn't interested in *him*. Fortunately her shrink was able to get to the bottom of her problems and she was last seen making an attempt to relate to men—look-alikes or not—according to who they were, not by qualities she affixed to them.

Moderation is probably the answer. But make sure you pursue all possibilities whether he's your type or not.

3. Pursue the Fantasy Man

It's a free evening. Memories of your courtship blur your vision as you try to read the bestseller list. Even a hot bath doesn't sooth your nerves. You can't turn your mind off the silence of the house (the kids are sleeping).

Well, there *is* something to do. Most women I talked to met men while they were married that interested them. But marriage prevented them from getting together. I propose now's the time to take the risk and find him. *Here's how:*

1. Make a list of all the men you met in the last year before the separation. Turn over in your mind all the

places you've been—parties, meetings, dinners, weddings, graduations—and remember the men. List them all. For a moment just forget their qualifications or lack of. Just get the entire list.

2. Study the list carefully. And then check off the names of those who, now admit it, turned you on to thoughts of passion, lovemaking, or even gave you a faint tingle of anticipation as they said goodnight to you.

3. Make a separate list of these "fantasy" men with answers to these questions:

> Where did you meet him?
> What did he look like?
> Why do you remember him?
> Was he married, single, or divorced?
> What does he do?
> What did he seem most interested in talking about?

Add any other notations that would give you a clue to finding him and having him discover you.

Ready for the next step?

4. Change fantasy into fact; daydreams into action. Go out, using every bone of wile, every hair of courage, and don't rest until you find a way to contact him. If you're worried about being rejected, it's highly unlikely: most men are interested in you if you are interested enough in them to make the first move. My list included Peter S. and Paul D.

Peter S.
Met at Sally's house for dinner (loves corn on the cob).
Sally's cousin.
Lives in Vermont.
Blue eyes—looks like a cross between Joe Namath and Dustin Hoffman.
Has a girl friend—no competition.
Told me my skirt was too short. Could swear he was turned on.

All I did was call Sally and ask her about that dinner party. I reminisced with her and told her I remembered the food to this day (it had been quite a feast). This naturally led to her cousin: he had brought fresh fruits and vegetables from Vermont. After commentary about the relative natural produce, Sally told me she was going to Vermont the following weekend, and then: "Would you like to drive up with me? I'd love the company." It was settled. I was off to the woods and within twenty-four hours of breathing fresh air, he and I were in the woods together making love on cool patches of lawn in a meadow. We water-skied in our birthday suits, the erotic sensation of the wind and water whirling around our bodies; we drank tequila, sucked lemons and licked salt in his isolated cabin until dawn; we made love by the light of a kerosene lamp; and we mutually satisfied a hunger for intimacy.

So those feelings I had had at Sally's dinner party weren't all one sided after all.

Paul D.
Always at Brenda's office when I met her for lunch.
Admissions officer at college.
He laughed a lot.
Has big beard—nice hands—very tall.

Since Brenda was single and her head was into dating, I didn't have to be coy. I asked her right out. "Would you help me?"

We figured that if I met Paul again at her office, I should be open about my interest in him. In fact, we would invite him to lunch with us. She knew that he had some research to do in their library the following Tuesday. So that Tuesday I dressed in my most alluring collegiate slacks and sweater—some of my friends call it my cheerleader look, but if I was into any leading it wasn't on the football field.

We went to lunch as planned. He was even better than I thought. We all parted with promises to lunch together again. I even felt he would call me. Guess again. He called Brenda and asked her to dinner; end of my story. She called me later and thanked me . . . he was terrif in bed. Well, if I didn't get the benefit of his study in Sweden (he had been in school there for

202

years and then taught), at least one of my dearest friends could.

Lists can and should be made—literally or mentally. Here's what can happen.

Dolores went after her old beau. Not a bad idea. How many women will admit to their fantasies about that one guy in their lives whom they left to get married? Before saying "I do" there is usually one man who stands out as a possible choice. Having said no to him, getting married to someone else usually brings about some feelings of: Have I done the right thing? I should never have married George (now the ex). I wonder where he (the old beau) is now? Is he married? Happy? Dolores found out the answers to these questions:

"I remember Charles. I couldn't really remember it all, but we used to laugh a lot, talk about the future, solve world problems, and drink, and have a college good time. We dated the third year in college. Our senior year we drifted apart. After school was over I moved to San Francisco—the teacher bit. He was from L.A. I wrote him that I wasn't going back to Chicago, where my family was. I saw him in San Francisco. He came up for a weekend. Sort of conservative, he was shocked by the way I lived.

"We had a lovely old apartment, smoked pot, and generally did what we wanted—not what our parents wanted or society. He was definitely society's child. By now he was a lawyer and a good one. I was confused. I liked my life but I was living in two worlds —teacher, just what my parents wanted, dated lawyers and residents at the hospital. But then there was another side of me that couldn't stand the conventions of this world . . . the lack of fun . . . the values of she's a nice girl, he's a nice boy, he makes a lot of money. I preferred the artists, the would-be filmmakers, the writers who seemed to care more about people and enjoying themselves than about what people said about them. The weekend with Charles was the . . . well . . . it really pointed out how different my life was gradually moving since I had left. We drank, we talked, and I realized now that Charles just thought it was a phase of mine. He thought I should let my father give me money, I should then be a social worker, and then marry well, whatever that means. He stayed the weekend and I remember spending a lot of time in bed. He could still press the right buttons to my satisfaction. Then the man I ultimately married came along. A filmmaker. Tony and I lived together for two years before we got married. We were married for two years. I don't regret a thing now, but the last few months of my marriage I couldn't help thinking about Charles. Maybe he was right, maybe I couldn't take the freer life of the filmmaker, the ups and downs of his career, the forays into the unusual. I thought of him many times, lonely without my husband around. So what if Charles was a little conservative? Maybe I was too. Didn't I cringe every time something stronger than pot appeared on the scene? Sex, by the way, turned from the fun and adventurous to the mundane. Lots of things went wrong. Maybe it was my inability to decide who I was. We divorced.

"Shortly afterward, I went to a cocktail party, wondering why I bothered to go, felt very very lonely, and got involved in a conversation with some casual acquaintances. They were gossiping about the good old days at school—when we all attended Northwestern. Charles's name came up. I couldn't believe that after all these years I would be hearing about him. Then I heard that he had married and was divorced. That night I went home and had a long conversation with the telephone operator from Denver, Colorado. Where would a bachelor who liked the finer things in life live in Denver? We managed to narrow it down to three numbers (his last name was common). I found him all right, and that weekend I was on the plane to Denver (at his expense). I was scared but I was willing to see what I had turned down in favor of my husband, soon to become a memory.

"We toasted our reunion and plop—we were in bed. This man who turned me on over and over, was NOT the same man I remembered. But obviously he was the same. I had changed. He was so conservative (at least

204

I can say that my husband was adventurous) and I had had the benefit of a little variety since my separation. Charles didn't enjoy sex. I couldn't believe it. He was as conservative in bed as he was playing the stock market.

"Let me give you an example: when I started to go down on him he pushed me away and said, 'I like that, but not now. I'll tell you when' . . . and he never did. And later, when I tried again, 'I'm not a prude. I really like it.' Anyone who has to tell me he's not a prude is one. And I stopped trying.

"I left Denver that weekend feeling liberated. Even though my marriage was over, I had married the right man for me at the time. And I certainly was better off than if I had married Charles. I knew who I was—somewhere in between Charles's rigid code of ethics and my husband's careless ways. I was lucky."

Not everyone is lucky enough to find her ex-lover and have him so readily available. But if it's possible, give it a try. Even if he is married, have lunch with him. Chances are he's nothing like you remember, and you'll realize you are finally liberated from that romantic dream.

A word of caution: there is always a catch-22 to every calculated plan. You might rekindle feelings of yours, but he may find you as boring as your cousin's piano recital.

Linda added "no-name" and Bill B. She had mentally made a list of men she was interested in pursuing and came up with two real possibilities—she thought.

No-name
Has cocky smile . . . studied manner.
Did political work on last political campaign.
Wears tight pants, has blond hair.
Reads French plays and German philosophers.

"I didn't know anything about this man. He was terrific-looking—sex was his middle name. The first thing I did was call the campaign headquarters where we had both been working. I volunteered my services to help with an 'issues' mailing the candidate was sending out. Since he was an incumbent there was always work to do around his office—even if it wasn't election time.

"I went there and typed addresses and licked stamps for six weeks, twice a week, before I found out Sexy No-Name was Joe C. And he was living with a scrumptious blonde who 'made him happy.' I mentally wished them well, and that was it for my stamp licking.

"When I gave up on Joe, however, I looked around the room and rediscovered a dear shy older man who had offered me rides home these past six weeks. Once we even stopped for coffee. He was recently divorced after twenty years of marriage, probably twenty years older than me, and very nice. The night of the revelation he drove me home and knew I was upset. He was kind and I finally told him how lonely I was. He suggested a drink instead of coffee. Just what I needed. Two hours later, my life story in front of us and four brandy alexanders, and I invited him to stay the night with me.

"The combination must have been right because I had the best orgasm in the four months since divorce—and I know he enjoyed himself—it was an inspired blow-job, if I do say so myself.

"We parted the next morning both knowing we wouldn't see each other again. That night was something special. It would never be repeated."

Bill B.
Met at dance without his wife.
House guest of Sanders.
Lives in L.A., but spends a lot of time in the East; obviously travels a lot.
Body in great shape. Good color sense with clothes: red cashmere sweater.

"A wonderful man who traveled a great deal, that's what the Sanders told me one afternoon. I had called them and invited myself for Sunday brunch. I purposely told both of them about my interest in Bill. This way I wouldn't have to risk upsetting Jane or David. I didn't want him to be envious, her to be jealous. They were close friends and I could ask questions directly. I found out that Bill was in therapy, had been married, was divorced, didn't seem like he was going to remarry, and was really a good person.

"I mentioned that he was very nice to me the time I met him—the time my husband made a fool of himself being nasty to me and flirting with his date to boot. Sure enough: about three weeks later I got a call from Bill. We met for dinner and talked for hours. He made it quite clear he was unattached and that his future plans did not include marriage. His wife had up and left him with no warning—and he was scarred. We went to his hotel room, ordered champagne from room service, watched the late movie on TV, and took a bubble bath together. We laughed and laughed. I remember washing him; I remember him drying me. And I remember being very very nervous all of a sudden. I really liked him. He knew I was nervous. I was shy. He gave me a warm hug, left the room, and came back with a bottle of talc. He gently pushed me on the bed. Then slowly and gently he smoothed powder all over my body. I was relaxed knowing he cared if I felt good. There wasn't a part of my body he didn't touch . . . my neck, my eyes, my breasts, my nipples, arms, stomach, the crease behind my knees, the outer layers of my vagina, my mound of hair, buttocks, thighs, my legs, and my toes. Wow. I hadn't received such attention in years. My clit was vibrating. I was weak and helpless. I turned over to look at him. He was hard and stiff. I reached for him; suddenly I was no longer nervous or shy. I felt warm throbbing flesh. I licked his cock from bottom to top; slowly and around. I caressed his balls. Then I opened my mouth wide, and took his wet delicious penis into my mouth. He shuddered. UP and down. It was yummy good. I got on top of him and much to my surprise hardly began to move, I came. He moved inside of me and exploded there. I couldn't wait to start all over again. And did.

207

"Later, Bill's lean blond body stretched out next to mine became one of my favorite daydreams.

"We see each other about once a week. And we are good friends. And we are satisfied lovers. Neither of us are ready to get married. Although we both have been divorced for some time now, neither of us is really interested—yet—in marriage. So it's perfect."

Linda had one major failure and one major success. She and Bill are now living together and getting the most from their relationship.

Miranda, living in New York, worked in the advertising business. Despite her access to the "man's world," she told me she sat down and made a list of all the possibilities. Here are two of them:

Jack C.
Gladys introduced us. Used to be her boyfriend.
Works in publishing.
Wears glasses . . . serious.
Did he have a nose job?

"Worked in the publishing business. That was little enough to go on. Gladys had moved to California. I could have called her there but decided against it; she really would have been on the phone in a minute telling everyone I was interested in her discards. Better, I called a friend of hers; we talked of Gladys's wedding and it was natural that Jack's name would come up. And just as naturally I asked her what publishing company he worked for. The rest was simple: I devised this marvelous idea for a book and called him about it. He immediately suggested lunch. That's all I got was lunch. And his dirty vulgar mouth with innuendos over the vichyssoise. I couldn't wait to get away from him. I guess he had looked better to me when all I had going for me were my daydreams. But at least I know why Gladys went back to her old beau so fast. I only wonder what took her so long."

Miranda had better luck with Sam G.

Sam G.
At Sylvia's wedding. Friend of the groom.
Quiet. Strong. Great eyes. About fifty years old.
Experienced. Commanded attention (he got mine).

"Tracking down Sam was the most difficult of all the men on my list. I gave up a number of times. But when I was bored (usually late at night), I made up lists of ways to find him. I did call Sylvia about him but she could barely remember whom I was talking about. She promised to ask her husband; he was really a business friend of his. Whether she did or not I'll never know. I do remember from our conversation that he traveled a lot—some kind of oil negotiations. Then one day I picked up a magazine and it was an interview with his wife—at one of their homes. And there he was at home with wife. The article said that the couple lived there and entertained happily. Crushed. But then I began to scan magazines and newspapers for more on this couple. Most of what I saw was her at this affair, that function, and usually with escort but not Sam. And in one place I read this was his third marriage and of course there were lots of children from them all. And then I saw him in columns—always with a different woman. When he was in New York I always went to the restaurant or theater he had been to. Kind of fruitless—something like closing the barn door after the fire. But it did give me a point of view.

"Then, returning from a short flight to a printing plant for the company I worked for, I landed at Kennedy instead of La Guardia. I saw a commotion at the end of the luggage pick-up. Just annoyed at having landed farther away from home, I moved toward the doors to get a taxi. Then I saw: the center of attraction was Samuel G. A man who never traveled without lawyers, etc.

"At least I had my wits about me. I moved through all the people and walked right up to him and introduced myself. Oh, my god, there was the smile again. But this time I smiled back. He was surprised. His eyes wrinkled in appreciation. I knew I would see him again.

209

There is nothing like the style of the older man. He really knows how to make you feel like a woman. A week later to the day I opened the door and there were a dozen white roses. Lovely. And always something every week for eleven weeks. And finally: he called. He would be arriving from L.A. that night. Would I have dinner with him?

"Would I? He was perfect. He had his interests, his wife, his oil. I just wanted his attention as a great lover with no demands and lots of experience.

"From the minute we met again he began asking questions about me. He was one of those men who really wanted to know about me and about my divorce (more on that later). He was kind, he gave me some good advice, and he ordered a marvelous dinner. Nothing like a delicious dinner and fine wine to make me feel sexy. So we went back to the apartment he was using while he was in the city. In fact, for the next two weeks, the two of us were inseparable. It was a wonderful feeling; being with a man for fourteen days, knowing that I would be able to walk into a room with a man; knowing where I would be every night; knowing who would be in my bed every night and every morning. All this was the first time I had been with one man for more than three days since my divorce. And it felt divinely wonderful. And the best part of it was the fact that I knew he would be leaving and that I needn't worry that this would interfere with my Operation Experiment. After all, I had only been divorced three months at this time and anything more permanent would have been fatal. Sammie knew this and when we were together he was careful never to mention the future and he was attentive and devoted at the present. When he finally left for Brazil I cried for two days because the emptiness in my stomach actually hurt. But gradually I had my memories and I got myself together to face the next man on my list."

Shelly tried and at first the gods weren't with her. It did give her some experience in the school of hard work, however. Her list included Melvin S., David G., and George R.

Melvin S.
Saw him at artist loft.
In movies or TV.
Danced gorgeously; fantastic body . . . he could move.

"I tried and tried to find him but no one knew anything about him. I called the artist who had the party at his loft. He only knew him as a filmmaker with address unknown. I often think of Melvin to this day, but I have never seen him since that night. (He did make a movie; it got good reviews and didn't make much money.) Pity I haven't run into him. If he moved as well in bed as he did on the dance floor, then it might have been a lovely romance!"

But that didn't stop her from pursuing David G.

David G.
Met at July 4th celeb last year, with Zimmers.
Had a date; don't think his wife.
On the make.
Gave me a big hug, with meaning, I thought, when he left.

"I called the Zimmers and found out that David was not married and was very much available. He didn't even have a steady girl friend. I told them I was definitely interested. About a week later I received the call. 'Just divorced?' he opened. I should have known then what kind of man he was but I agreed to see him after work that day. I guess I was really feeling lonely and those hours between work and home seemed to be the hardest to face.

"My first thought when I saw him was that he wasn't as sexy as I had remembered. But I tried to be nice. After all, he'd called me because I instigated it. Nice, I repeat. Not even flirtatious. But my memory did serve me loud and clear on another aspect of David: he was on the make all right. His hands kept wandering as he talked: hands on thigh to express lust; on arm for intimacy; on face for seriousness; on hand for sadness; and you're not going to believe this, brushing breast when excited. And he managed to run the gamut of emotions in the hour we sat there and I felt like a book written in braille. When he made the lunge for my left breast, that was it; I made a lunge for his cock, tweaked it. When he thought that was a measure of my desire, I should have known. I wish I could have said I left then. But I didn't. I found myself in bed with him three hours later. I just didn't think about who he was. Hopefully his boudoir manners would be better than his dining habits. Wrong. He wouldn't get it up. Really couldn't. And then he blamed me. So I worked on him. I gave him head, stroked his penis. He'd get hard and then when he came close to getting near my cunt, he'd wilt. After an hour of this I suggested his leaving. Actually I told him to go. It was useless and I was disgusted with myself. He left. So much for being aggressive."

However, she persevered and finally aggressive positive behavior paid off with George R.

George R.
Friend of husband's best friend.
Heavy into therapy.
A lawyer.
Very positive person.
Looks early thirties, but probably into forties.
Has nice laugh.

"I met him the night eight of us had dinner at a new French restaurant. Clearly, I needed some clever method to find this man. But how in the world was I going to get to my husband's best friend's friend. Never fear. When there is a male around worth pursuing, there are ways to get to him. I did know that he was a lawyer in town and that he had gone to Greece for a holiday. I had two clues here: I could call him and ask him about hotels in Athens, say I needed a lawyer desperately for something or other.

I had just had an encounter with a professional divorcee dater and I had to wash the taste out of my mouth. So: I phoned his office, asked his secretary to put him on the line, and when he said hello, I blurted: 'I met you with Arthur and Alex at Pierre's about six months ago; in fact, I used to be married to Alex and he's Arthur's best friend, did you have a good time in Greece; in fact, you're the most sexy man I ever met.' I froze. What did I say? He laughed. 'Good. Let's have drinks.' I couldn't believe it. Success, so far.

"He picked me up and we talked and talked and talked. Since we were both in therapy at the time it seemed that all kinds of pomp and circumstances could be eliminated. I felt I had known him for years. He told me he was seeing a woman whom he planned to marry. I was disappointed but somehow it didn't matter that night. I invited him back to my place after dinner —drinks turned into a luxurious dinner—and of course he accepted. With a light kiss on my nose. We took a cab to my place and went upstairs. All the way in the taxi he was fondling my breasts. By the time we got upstairs I was wet between the legs.

"But he was not the only one who could tantalize. I managed to rub and stroke his penis so that it was firm and erect.

"Then, with an abrupt movement, the evening turned into sweat and passion. I frankly don't even remember getting undressed. I do remember our slippery bodies making lustful noises as we came together. He was incredible. We made love at least four times that night. I could barely walk the next morning.

"That was my first and last night with him. He was about to be married. But I knew I was a woman. And that was the name of the game. We meet for lunch frequently and have become confidants. Every woman needs a man to hold her hand as she tries to pull her life together. George was perfect. We could flirt—we had already slept together so somehow flirting was enough. There was enough sex in the air to provide tension but it wasn't necessary to act on it. We had been intimate and now we just felt good being with each other.

Arleen had her say.

"After the divorce, I experimented like crazy. God, what I didn't do. Then all of a sudden I stopped. I was into other things; the men came as a matter of course. Then when Jake came along, I knew he was the man I wanted to marry." She told me he certainly fell into the category of seek-and-ye-shall-be-rewarded (hopefully) men."

Casper's father:
Didn't know his name.
Was at PTA meeting.
A widower (I asked at the time why he was alone).
Greg will know who he is . . . he has son Greg's age.

"Casper's father was a widower. That much I knew. I got this information from my son, Greg, who was in Casper's class at school. When I asked Greg Casper's father's name, of course Greg didn't know. Casper called him Dad. Then I decided that all that TV watching had finally been worthwhile. What would Doris Day have done? Simple: I encouraged Greg to invite Casper for dinner. That accomplished, I tried to draw out Casper about his father. I found out he could throw a ball farther, was bigger than, caught more fish than, and could kick a football better than any other father. And Casper was no help: he was more interested in Greg's aquarium. I left it there. Greg, although eleven years old, was pretty hip. And I didn't need any interference there; even his help would be too much. So I planned alone. I really sound like a scheming person but with all the time on my hands late at night made me resolve to try this once to get what I wanted.

"Finally I decided to take Greg on a short camping trip. And naturally we decided to ask Casper if he wanted to come. For this, I needed permission. And by then I knew Casper's father's name. Jake. He was delighted at the suggestion. He would have some time to himself. So Jake arrived on Saturday and deposited Casper at our house with all the equipment. If this were romantic fiction then I would tell you that Jake took one look at me in my Levis and sweatshirt and decided then and there he had never seen me before as a woman and announced he was coming with us and the four of us lived happily ever after.

"What actually happened was a long one-sided thank you. Jake was indebted to me: now he could spend the entire weekend with his girl friend. He'd do the same for me sometime. Terrific, I thought to myself. With whom?

"We actually had a good time, the three of us. We spent four days together. About a week after the trip, Jake dropped by to tell me Casper was still talking about the trip. He also told me all about his weekend. He was very taken with this girl. Well, it took three months of listening to Jake talk about his girl friend. The four of us had dinner together more and more. Then Jake would take off to see *that woman*—as I began to think of her. It was discouraging but I couldn't give up those dinners we had.

"Finally the four of us went camping. He was still playing big brother to me. After the trip, the conversations changed. I heard less about his plans for the future and we just relaxed and enjoyed ourselves.

"The evening I realized things changed between us was the night we spent together. By then the boys were so used to seeing the two of us together, neither of them questioned it.

"As you know, we are married now, and I'm expecting another child."

Arleene's story has a happy ending for her. Marriage was her goal. She had been divorced three years by the time she married Jake (it took her two years to get him to realize they were practically living together).

Never be in the position of having failed without trying. These women tried and were accepted, sought after, and dumped on. But none of them would ever have to say, "Well, if I had only . . ." and feel that they had lost out of something good.

Pursuing men in an intelligent way is a perfectly normal healthy way to conduct your social life. Sometimes I think there are nine million beautiful women for every one attractive man. So, you have to have the edge to even get him to look at you: often that edge is your interest. He may just respond to your positive attitude while the competition is playing cool (and giving him insecure feelings, no doubt). And then once the two of you have connected, it's up to you to make him forget that dark-haired beauty with the ideal measurements.

X.

Warning, Responsibilities and Hope

Warning

Old habits die hard and if you are a recently separated woman, there is one habit that you must break, if you have the inclination, and that's expecting too much from your new beau—or full-time attention. You have to keep in mind, no matter how good it may be between you and him, that he had a life before you arrived on the scene. In addition, it is sometimes far too easy to latch on to a man and think: "This is it. And it'll solve all my problems and I won't have to date, sleep with anyone else again. We'll live happily ever after (or even if it's second best, it's better than the loneliness)." It just doesn't work that way. (And remember, even if he is terrific, don't fall into the real domestic trap—living together, doing his laundry, making his meals, you're not ready for that yet).

Ronnie was hurt, disappointed, and miserable when George left her on Sunday morning after spending a fabulous night with her. She had just assumed they'd be together all day. Assumed. That's the word. Never assume.

"I had it all planned. George and I would go out to dinner and then back to my place. I made sure the icebox was full of goodies for breakfast and even dinner the next day. I even put clean sheets on the bed. My whole day was spent filled with the expectation of a night of fulfillment and loving. It was even better than I dreamed. We cuddled together to watch the morning sunrise and made love again and again. I forgot my problems and the world. We had breakfast in bed and I thought it would last forever—at least the day. Then he brushed my hair off my face and said he had to leave. He was taking his kids to the circus. My reaction: rejection. My words: angry. My feelings: hurt. I knew George had kids and was devoted to them but I just expected that he and I were together—like it was with my husband. Sundays were always ours to do nothing together. I didn't realize I would have to share him. When he left I tried to read the paper but kept thinking about George. By afternoon I felt really terrible. Not because he left. That had gone. But because I had made such a scene. After all, I reasoned, he knew his kids before he knew me. And I had had him all night."

Joyce wasn't so smart. As soon as she found Al, she started to make demands on him that were unfair and presumptuous.

"I just fell into old habits of being married. I just assumed that if he felt like spending a night with me, he would take on the full responsibility of me. If not that, then at least see only me. It was crazy and I realize now I was just falling into the habit of the man takes care of certain things. I assumed we'd do everything together. And when he'd call and say he had other plans, I'd hit the ceiling. The last row we had was on a Saturday morning when he left my bed and said he'd see me next week. I had assumed if he was going to see me on Friday, it would be the whole weekend. I made a scene. I was awful. And he never did call again."

In both cases, Ronnie and Joyce were counting on their intimacy of one night to extend to the next day (or weekend)—as if they were married. It was sometime in the sexual recovery period before Joyce realized that she had to break old habits; fortunately Ronnie saw things clearly before too much damage was done to a budding relationship.

Kathie's possessiveness broke up what might have been something special if she had allowed time for things to develop.

"I had been seeing Al for about a month. It was three months exactly after the divorce. I had been with a few men and nothing clicked. But with Al, it was different. I really think we had something special. But I blew it. I was so anxious to stop all that dating, fucking, etc., I put too many demands on him. I just assumed I belonged to him and he belonged to me. And by that it meant doing everything together. But that wasn't what he had in mind. And it all blew up over his season's football tickets. He had no intention of taking me since he got them every year with the same bunch of guys. I was pissed about this and just couldn't take it as anything but rejection. Two scenes and that was it. He called me possessive and walked out. But my husband had always included me in all his activities so I thought that was what it meant when you started seeing someone you liked."

Kathie has more than possessiveness as her problem. That her husband didn't have his *own* activities says something about their marriage. That she only saw herself as an extension of the man she was with had been nurtured by her marriage. That she found a guy who thought differently threw her off-balance. Kathie told me that it took many more months before she was an independent person who had her activities and the man in her life would have his; and when they got together, they were then a couple. And it didn't need to be on a twenty-four-hour daily basis. She learned that independence is essential for her to be a whole person, to let him be a complete person, and finally the commitment between the two of them would be fuller.

Responsibilities

The yes, thanks—no thanks syndrome . . . How many times have you spent a night with a guy, just once, and that would have sufficed . . . in other words, you are no longer interested. It doesn't matter the reason: he was perfectly dreadful or there was just no chemistry. But he still pursues you. Faced with saying no after saying yes, that one time, often panics the DW who is still groping for the ground rules of her new life. Some women have confessed that's easier to say yes than no. It's after the second yes that you will hate yourself in the morning. Once you catch on, however, there are any number of ways of avoiding the situation in the future. The point is to deal with it immediately. Don't let the idea that he'll be hurt, you'll be all alone once again, or he'll think you were terrible to say yes the first time, stop you from saying loud and clear: NO. You have to live with yourself. And you are more important than what he thinks of you.

Don't give in to the panic or desperation of loneliness and say yes. Liz told me just after her divorce was final that she went to a party and was feeling very depressed. "I went to this party and the first man that looked at me twice didn't have a chance. I was all over him. We went back to my place. That night. He was very sweet but really an inattentive lover. Very selfish. It turned out to be awful. I vowed never to do it again. But the next time he called, he was very sweet on the phone and I was lonely and I figured I should give him another chance. That night after he fell asleep satisfied, I was too hung up to sleep, I thought: 'How did I let this happen to me: I had traded a lonely evening for one of self-disgust and felt more lonely than ever.' Next time it was easy to say no and I felt much better about myself. I felt so virtuous that I actually enjoyed watching TV that night and washing my hair."

It's a trap every woman falls into. But fortunately it's one you can avoid eventually if you're willing to say no.

At the same time you have to remember that no man has a claim on you any longer. Just because you meet a man, enjoy his company, and sex turns out to be super fantastic, it doesn't mean that he has any right to demand full-time attention from you. (That it feels good to have this attention can't be denied, but remember, at this time you must not settle into one relationship.)

There were many times during the six-month period when all I wanted to do was crawl into bed . . . alone. If that sounds contradictory to what I have been saying, let me clear up any confusion. Socializing is healthy. But at the same time it's my choice when, how, and where. And by the same token, it's my choice to say no. I am obligated to no one.

If saying no to the man you are seeing is taken as total rejection, it's time you reconsider where his head is at. It's also a time to consider how you say no. And if you still think you have made it clear that you like him and enjoy him and you still want some time to yourself, and he still makes a scene, you have no choice but to cross him off your list as an eligible playmate. It's no time to have to ward off possessiveness, is it?

You may enjoy the dinner but want to go home to wash your hair, organize your thoughts, and prepare yourself to face the next day. Maybe you just want to read a good book. That's your decision, isn't it? It's mine. (By the way, the same holds true for him; if he drops you off without coming in, don't take it as the end of the world when he tells you he's going home because he has to be up at seven-thirty the next day for an important meeting. This works both ways, you know.)

Furthermore, just because you spent the night with him and want to see him again, it doesn't mean you can't refuse him to go out with someone else. If he starts asking questions, and wants to put in a total claim for you, you'd better straighten him out fast.

Hope

If you are lucky enough to find the "right" guy the first time, be careful. He likes you; you like him. You both like sex . . . with each other.

However, don't make it a steady thing with him. You've just gotten a divorce. You haven't even given yourself a chance to see who you are now that you are an independent woman. The scars of marriage and separation are deeper than you can see. It can take years for them to properly heal. Don't mess it up by turning domestic with the first man who turns you on.

What's good now might not be that great later, as you give yourself a chance to experiment with other men and get used to your new life as a divorced woman. You need time to get over the marriage in order to judge any new relationship. For now, the security of having a man around who cares can overshadow every other consideration. If you settle now, you may be settling for less.

There are ways of keeping men interested even if you are not ready to make any commitment about the relationship. But if you have just gotten divorced, don't start visualizing wedding bells for the two of you, yet. After all, you're barely out of the virginal phase.

And for the doubter in the crowd who asks: What if you're very lucky and he's terrific with and for you;

might this casual view just mess things up? That question can only come from someone who has never been divorced. After a marriage breaks up there must be a proper mourning period before settling into a permanent relationship again. Your divorce is giving you a new lease on life. It's time to be an independent woman experiencing life to its fullest—and that includes experimenting with a variety of men. And finally it's your chance to decide what your lifestyle will be for you (and your children, if you've got them). And who knows, you may decide never to remarry—just have a series of lovers. And why not? If you decide to get married, there's a better chance it will be a full relationship based on two people working together to make it work.